The Year of the Poet XII

October 2025

The Poetry Posse

inner child press, ltd.
'building bridges of cultural understanding'

The Poetry Posse 2025

Gail Weston Shazor
Shareef Abdur Rasheed
Teresa E. Gallion
hülya n. yılmaz
Noreen Snyder
Tzemin Ition Tsai
Elizabeth Esguerra Castillo
Jackie Davis Allen
Mutawaf Shaheed
Caroline 'Ceri' Nazareno
Ashok K. Bhargava
Alicja Maria Kuberska
Swapna Behera
Albert 'Infinite' Carrasco
Kimberly Burnham
Eliza Segiet
William S. Peters, Sr.

~ * ~

In order to maintain each poet's authentic voice, this volume has not undergone the scrutiny of editing. Please take time to indulge each contributor for their own creativity and aspirations to convey their uniqueness.

hülya n. yılmaz, Ph.D.
Director of Editing ~
Inner Child Press International

General Information

The Year of the Poet XII
October 2025 Edition

The Poetry Posse

1st Edition : 2025

This Publishing is protected under Copyright Law as a "Collection". All rights for all submissions are retained by the Individual Author and or Artist. No part of this Publishing may be Reproduced, Transferred in any manner without the prior **WRITTEN CONSENT** of the "Material Owners" or its Representative Inner Child Press. Any such violation infringes upon the Creative and Intellectual Property of the Owner pursuant to International and Federal Copyright Laws. Any queries pertaining to this "Collection" should be addressed to Publisher of Record.

Publisher Information
1st Edition : Inner Child Press
intouch@innerchildpress.com
www.innerchildpress.com

Copyright © 2025 : The Poetry Posse

ISBN-13 : 978-1-961498-74-7 (inner child press, ltd.)

$ 12.99

WHAT WOULD LIFE BE WITHOUT A LITTLE POETRY?

Dedication

This Book is dedicated to

Humanity, Peace & Poetry

the Power of the Pen

can effectuate change!

&

The Poetry Posse

past, present & future,

our Patrons and Readers &

the Spirit of our Everlasting Muse

*In the darkness of my life
I heard the music
I danced...
and the Light appeared
and I dance*

Janet P. Caldwell

Table of Contents

Foreword ... ix

Preface ... xi

Emotions ... xiii

Anticipation ~ Pride ~ Regret

The Poetry Posse

Gail Weston Shazor	1
Alicja Maria Kuberska	9
Jackie Davis Allen	15
Tzemin Ition Tsai	23
Noreen Snyder	29
Elizabeth Esguerra Castillo	35
Mutawaf Shaheed	41
hülya n. yılmaz	49
Teresa E. Gallion	57
Ashok K. Bhargava	63
Caroline Nazareno-Gabis	71
Swapna Behera	77

Table of Contents . . . *continued*

Albert Carassco	83
Kimberly Burnham	87
Eliza Segiet	93
William S. Peters, Sr.	99

October's Featured Poets — 107

Фросина Тасевска	109
Tanja Ajtic	115
Jerome L. Duque	123
Priyanka Neogi	129

Inner Child Press News — 139

Other Anthological Works — 185

Foreword

Anticipation ~ Pride ~ Regret

On behalf of our brother in letters Shareef

I truly believe that lowering one's expectations, will reduce the anxiety of anticipation. Taking the middle course in all of life's affairs can thwart feelings of despair and major let downs. Pride interferes with taking the time to understand real time circumstances, thus limiting the misgivings and mistakes one commits in putting too much emphasis in the self. Insecurities can also be disguised as false pride. The lack of humility leads to arrogance, that in turn leads to many disasters and mistakes. As a human being you will always make mistakes, but coming to terms with them is where pride can become fatal. Making informed decisions, being patient and cautious, listening to those who have stood the test of time, These, are some of the tools I feel can be used to also reduce many regrets one faces. On occasions there should not be any regrets depending on what the event was that happened. How does one classify regret? Be careful in what one pursues and desires. Regret can become a permeant fixture in a person's life.

Proet Mutawaf Shaheed

Now Available
www.innerchildpress.com

Preface

We, **Inner Child Press International, The Year of the Poet** and **The Poetry Posse** welcome you.

As we now closing in on the end of our 12th year of monthly publications for **The Year of the Poet**, we continue to be excited.

This particular year we have chosen to feature a collection of human emotions. We do hope you enjoy the poet's perspectives on these subjects. Read ~ Learn.

For those of you who are not familiar with our story, back in 2013, a few of us poets got together with the simple intention of producing a book a month. That was our challenge. Since that time the enterprise has blossomed and brought forth a fruit that seems to keep on growing as evidenced as we enter 2023.

Our purpose is simple. Through our lyrical words and verse, we not only wish to share our poetic works, but we also have the poetic naiveté to believe that we can assist in the growth of consciousness of the things that have an effect our collective humanity. Therefore, we welcome your readership. For more about what we are attempting to accomplish, have a look at our Publishing Web Site . . . www.innerchildpress.com. If you would like to

know a bit more about this particular endeavor please stop by for a visit at :
www.innerchildpress.com/the-year-of-the-poet

Over the years, Inner Child Press has been socially active to bring awareness and catalog through literature the things that have an impact upon our world and its inhabitants. We have solicited, produced, underwritten and published quite a few volumes to that end. For more insight you may wish to visit : www.innerchildpress.com/the-anthology-market. If you are a writer, poet, or activist, you would be advised to keep a eye out for upcoming volumes should you desire to participate. All readers are welcomed as well. Note, that there is a myriad of published volumes that are available as a FREE PDF download as well as available for purchase at affordable prices.

We at this time extend to you our well wishes for your own personal journey and hope that you consider including us as a travel companion.

Bless Up

Bill

William S. Peters, Sr.

Publisher
Inner Child Press International
www.innerchildpress.com

Anticipation ~ Pride ~ Regret

Anemone   Amaryllis   Purple Hyacinths

This October we consider anticipation or eagerly awaiting the future as well as the past in the theme of regret and pride or a feeling of accomplishment. The future or our anticipation of tomorrow, next Thanksgiving, an important birthday, the next poetry book are all in the future but on our minds right now. The successes and failures of the past also weigh on us encouraging us to stop for a moment in the here and now to bask in our accomplishments or vow to do better in ways that we have not reached the bar we have set for ourselves. Time and emotions interlace coloring how we feel about ourselves, our family and the world.

The tricky thing about time is to live into each moment with understanding of who we are and who we are connected to so that in the future we will have few regrets and much pride or satisfaction in our accomplishments. Mother Theresa said, "If we have no peace, it is because we have forgotten that we belong to each other." The same could be said about regrets, "if we have too many regrets, it is because we have forgotten that we belong to each other."

In The New Year Makes a Request, Abby E. Murray (Rattle, Jan, 2024) writes, "It wants us to stop wishing for peace like it's the one guarding some goldmine of surrender or compassion, like the act of not killing each other really is as easy as pouring tea into mugs... The new year is tossing our demands out the window like laundry, and here we are, ... we shriek. Who will bring us what we're waiting for?" In the comments Abby E. Murray says, "I imagine this new year as the mother of our future, listening to our prayers for peace that remain unfollowed by action. She wants us to get off our a** and make the peace we need ourselves."

I am struck by this line, "Who will bring us what we're waiting for?

And by a line from Beech Trees in Spring by James Crews. "I want to be like the maples, letting go so easily of their leaves in the slightest autumn breeze, surrendering every piece of themselves they no longer need, and embracing bareness like a new suit they can simply step into. But I'm more like the beech trees, which cling to the husks of their leaves long into spring."

I too want to be like the maple but fear I am more like the beech but with some introspection, a look at what I really want to hold onto, life, friendships, and peace, perhaps I will do more and hold on to less.

My wish for this fall season is that we all will find ways to have fewer regrets and actively do today what we can be proud of tomorrow.

Kimberly Burnham, PhD
(Integrative Medicine)
September, 2025 Spokane, WA & Portland, OR

Poets . . .
sowing seeds in the
Conscious Garden of Life,
that those who have yet to come
may enjoy the Flowers.

Poets, Writers . . . know that we are the enchanting magicians that nourishes the seeds of dreams and thoughts . . . it is our words that entice the hearts and minds of others to believe there is something grand about the possibilities that life has to offer and our words tease it forth into action . . . for you are the Poet, the Writer to whom the Gift of Words has been entrusted . . .

~ wsp

Poetry succeeds where instruction fails.

~ wsp

Open for Submissions

October 1st until December 31st

worldhealingworldpeace@gmail.com

Gail Weston Shazor

Gail Weston Shazor

Gail Weston Shazor is a lover of words. She is fond of the arcane, unusual and the not yet words.

Coining words at an early age, there was often a bit of trouble with teachers, but she always had her mother and aunt to back up her choices in expression. Born in Mississippi, she spent her early years with her grandparents. Each of the four left very careful influences on her pre-schooling. She learned in turn how women worked in and out of the home and how men worked in and out of the home to support the family. She learned that a lack of proper schooling was not the only way to learn and understanding life was a great teacher. As in most rural families of color, women had a greater chance of formal learning. Both of Gail's grandmothers read out loud to the family whether it was the bible or the newspapers and important documents to their spouses.

Gail Weston Shazor has authored (so far) Notes from the Blue Roof, A Overstanding of an Imperfect Love, HeartSongs and Lies My Grandfather's Told Me. The number of anthologies is too many to list with the premier accomplishment of one of the contributors to The Year of The Poet. Gail will always lend her ink to community projects and will purchase the books of fellow poets in the Inner Child Press family.

And a dream

Greying dreams transmute
Old memories into dust
Across still water
Drums always will beat
Requiring attention
Of a calling sound
The
Movement
Make cadence
Of the sounds
Gathered on the wind
The breath of whispering
And the black soil of the earth
The offering of new rainfalls
Until it is now in completion
I threw the jagged edges of the broken pieces
Into the rising sun

hanging up

The blood rushes to my head
And I find it hard to breathe
The aching and pain of a skull
Filled to bursting
With the blood of life
With the
Blood
Of
Death
And the smell
Of pretensions
Wafting through my ears
My ankles ache
From the chaffing of the bindings
Findings
Wanting
Needing
The lessening
From the chains pulling across bones
 Stretched to many limits of flesh
If I could just
Touch the ground with my fingertips
I might find a temporary relief
Outside my spirit woman
A tantalizing
And unfulfilling satiation
Much like a laden table with no salt
Tasteless
So I hang
And not as he hung
In perfection
But away from heaven

Unworthy to bear the fruit of a race
Cast into the branches
In places far from
Golgotha
For much the same earthbound reason
Fear
Reflecton
Hate
Each hair shirt heavier than the next
Worn uneasily
In desert heat and verdant forests
In cotton fields and steel mills
Even upside
Down
Here I hang
And my vision is finally clear

Dragons

To be able to sleep at night
I need to reconcile
The goings of the day
The silence is much more bearable
Than the untruths that
Have become the norm
My lies are no less pretentious
And far less pretty
For I act as if there
Is nothing wrong
When there is nothing right
The strain of going out
And coming in frays me
And I no longer want to
Be here in this space
Subjected to rules that belong
To no one else
And punishments that have
No basis in reality
And how did I become
The monster on everyone's shelf
For now, I will sleep
But even dragons awake once in a while

Gail Weston Shazor

Alicja Maria Kuberska

Alicja Maria Kuberska

Alicja Maria Kuberska – awarded Polish poetess, novelist, journalist, editor.

She is a member of the Polish Writers Associations in Warsaw, Poland and IWA Bogdani, Albania. She is also a member of directors' board of Soflay Literature Foundation, Our Poetry Archive (India) and Cultural Ambassador for Poland (Inner Child Press, USA)

Her poems have been published in numerous anthologies and magazines in : Poland, Czech Republic, Slovakia, Hungary,Ukraina, Belgium, Bulgaria, Albania, Spain, the UK, Italy, the USA, Canada, the UK, Argentina, Chile, Peru, Israel, Turkey, India, Uzbekistan, South Korea, Taiwan, China, Australia, South Africa, Zambia, Nigeria

She received two medals - the Nosside UNESCO Competition in Italy (2015) and European Academy of Science Arts and Letters in France (2017). Ahe also received a reward of international literary competition in Italy „ Tra le parole e 'elfinito" (2018). She was announced a poet of the 2017 year by Soflay Literature Foundation (2018).She also received : Bolesław Prus Prize Poland (2019), Culture Animator Poland (2019) and first prize Premio Internazionale di Poesia Poseidonia- Paestrum Italy (2019).

Spring is coming

It's time to wake up
the sleeping trees in orchards,
open the hives and welcome the bees,
invite the first flowers to the concert.

The hard-working insects
with golden wings
will play a wedding march in the sky.
They will make a mating flight
in honor of the queen.

A quiet buzzing will fill the space
the air will smell like honey
and the wind will chant the song

new life is coming
fertile summer is coming
autumn harvest is coming

Autumn love

You kissed me.
I felt a bittersweet taste in my mouth.
I closed my eyes.
In my imagination I saw the park.
Do you remember?
You said we were like two trees in autumn.

Look,
naive, youthful thoughts flew off
-frivolous, migratory birds.
The first chill chased them.
Their joyous trill,
glorifying a perfect love, rang out.
Delusions fell to the ground like leaves,
rotting and turning to dust.
We are firmly rooted in the soil of everyday life.

My angel

Forgive me the wounded feet.
You walk with me
through the wilderness ,
The thorns of sins tear at your robes.

You protect me against
the mud of evil words
and mean deeds.
You fight against perverse thoughts.

Thank you for faithful persistence,
for showing me the way in darkness
and sometimes lending me your wings.

Jackie Davis Allen

Jackie Davis Allen

Jackie Davis Allen, otherwise known as Jacqueline D. Allen or Jackie Allen, grew up in the Cumberland Mountains of Appalachia. As the next eldest daughter of a coal miner father and a stay at home mother, she was the first in her family to attend and graduate from college. Her siblings, in their own right, are accomplished, though she is the only one, to date, that has discovered the gift of writing.

Graduating from Radford University, with a Bachelor's of Science degree in Early Education, she taught in both public and private schools. For over a decade she taught private art classes to children both in her home and at a local Art and Framing Shop where she also sold her original soft sculptured Victorian dolls and original christening gowns.

She resides in northern Virginia with her husband, taking much needed get-aways to their mountain home near the Blue Ridge Mountains, a place that evokes memories of days spent growing up in the Appalachian Mountains.

A lover of hats, she has worn many. Following marriage to her college sweetheart, and as wife, mother, grandmother, teacher, tutor, artist, writer, poet and crafter, she is a lover of art and antiques, surrounding herself, always, with books, seeking to learn more.

In 2015 she authored *Looking for Rainbows, Poetry, Prose and Art*, and in 2017, *Dark Side of the Moon*. Both books of mostly narrative poetry were published by Inner Child Press and were edited by hulya n. yilmaz in 2019, *No Illusions. Through the Looking Glass*, which was nominated to be considered for a Pulitzer Prize by the publisher and editor of Inner Child Press, ltd.

http://www.innerchildpress.com/jackie-davis-allen.php
jackiedavisallen.com

Regret vs Gratitude

That which stings and hurts today
May direct you on to a better tomorrow.

Regrets are best left in the past:
It's a stumbling block to future success,
if carried on backs. Like a sack of bricks.
Too heavy a burden to be of any help.

Forgive yourself, others. Often.
Focus you energy away from regrets.

Seize opportunities for self-improvement:
Focus upon the here and now; and,
Remember that mistakes
Offer opportunities for reflection,

They're a means to change the direction.
That means there's more doors to open.

Invest in yourself. Try new things:
For a life filled with honor and respect,
Forgive others, often, and generously.
Think upon the positive. Not the negative.

Pursue creativity, dream your dreams.
Develop your gifts, talent, interests.

Fill up your life's cup. Better days will come:
Release old hurts; and again if necessary.
Pray for strength to improve your lot;
Nourish your body, listen to its needs.

Breathe in the best of life's offerings.
If you fall, get up and start over.

Forgive past weakness. Be brave.
Love your neighbor, yourself:
Failure, disappointment, requires,
reminds us to be gentle with ourselves.

The body follows the mind.
Its perfectly alright to ask for help.

Whatever happened, at the time,
may have seemed like the end of the world.
In the mirror of regret's emotion, the future
may reveal itself, beautifully transformed

Anticipation

I'm in love! I'm in love!
At least I think I am!
Never heard the term, "Puppy Love",
Wouldn't have believed it anyway!

I've wings on my feet!
I'm soaring through the air.
Everything's going my way,
I'm hanging on to his every word.

I'm in love! I'm in love!
I know it's true! Indeed it's true!
There's no one that makes me
Feel like he does!

The days stretch into months,
Almost a year has gone by.
He's about to graduate, and I,
I've still a year to go.

I'm a little anxious, a bit concerned.
I'm trying not to think about goodbyes.
No need to worry, what a surprise!
He just placed a ring on my finger!

Pride

Pauline and I, we teamed up
To make a pecan pie;
And hoped to get an "A"
On our cooking-class grade.

We assembled the ingredients,
Followed the recipe.
Placed it in the preheated oven.
And waited, afterwards, for it to cool.

Serving as waitresses, Pauline and I,
We served the pecan pie to the guests:
Our high school teaching staff.
We, most proud of our accomplishment!

To our dismay, we were shocked to see
No one was eating, enjoying the dessert.
Alas, informed by Ms Boynton, we'd left
Out an essential ingredient: Karo syrup.

Jackie Davis Allen

Tzemin Ition Tsai

Tzemin Ition Tsai

Dr. Tzemin Ition Tsai comes from the Republic of China(Taiwan). In addition to being a professor of literature at a university, he is more committed to writing poems, novels, and proses. He is also an editor of "Reading, Writing and Teaching" academic text, an International editor of "Contemporary dialogues" literary periodical in Macedonia, and Vice-Chairman of the International Jury of the SAHITTO INTERNATIONAL AWARD in Bangladesh, and a columnist for "Chinese Language Monthly" in Taiwan.

In a wide range of literary creations, he is particularly fond of interesting stories or novels, and writing articles or poems about the feelings of nature and human beings. He has won many national literary awards. His literary works have been anthologized and published in books, journals, and newspapers in more than 55 countries and have been translated into more than 24 languages.

When Spring Knocks at the Door

The Yangtze roars, ceaseless,
like a voice murmuring the old tales,
a river's breath asking softly:
Will tomorrow's waters shine more clear?
Beyond the horizon, peaks half-veiled,
await their unveiling.
In the morning mist, someone lifts a lantern,
listening for echoes of Qin bricks, Han tiles.
Blossoms, birds, the wind, and a fine spring rain
trace in the air an unfinished arc.
Plum buds tremble, not yet daring to open,
like a poet holding tight to secret thoughts.
At the threshold of time, gentle knocks,
again and again,
in hope that spring will push the door ajar.

The Moon Unread in Jiangnan

On crumbled walls and broken stones,
green grass clings to faded glory.
Who still remembers the lights of Chang'an?
Who still hears the sighs within a nomad's flute?
I walk the desolate Silk Road,
the camel bells long fallen silent,
only yellow sands recall
the lonely ones who never returned
from listening to the whisper of bamboos.
Regret, like a letter never sent,
its ink blotched and fading.
It is the moon in Tang poems,
never rising over Jiangnan.
History turns a page,
and voices fall away
like shards of shattered glass,
too sharp for the hand to gather,
too painful for the heart to forget.

Where Time Builds a Nation

Look,
the Great Wall winding across a thousand miles,
not mere stones upon stones,
but countless hands,
frost and storm hardened into veins of steel.
Look,
the Yellow River surges,
its muddy waves thunder with the chest of the ancients.
Though for a thousand years it changes its course,
it never surrenders its rush toward the sea.
From bamboo slips to paper scrolls,
from paper scrolls to lamplight study,
the brush has carved more than words,
it has etched the unyielding marrow
of a people unbroken.
Mountains rise, rivers fall,
and through the vastness of time
the spine remains straight,
like a pine defying snow.
Standing against the wind,
O world, behold!
Here, where time builds layer upon layer,
stands the ancient heart of China.

Noreen Snyder

Noreen Snyder

Noreen Ann Snyder has been writing since she was a teenager. She writes a variety of different topics. Her favorite poetic forms are Sonnets, Blitz, Haiku, Tanka, and Free Verse. She always learning different poetic forms.

Noreen Ann Snyder is a poet, writer, and an author of five books, (four books are co-authored with her late husband, Garry A. Snyder.) Her poetry is in several Inner Child Press Anthologies. She is the founder of The Poetry Club on Facebook.

Anticipation Is...

Anticipation is like
waiting eagerly
being excited for
the 100 Thousand Poets for Change.
Where poets recite
their poetry about change
on justice, peace, and sustainability.
Phenomenal, talented poets
around the world
and that is something
to get excited about,
to rejoice because we want
to make a difference in this world.
We stand for change.
We stand for the voiceless.
We stand for you and me,
we stand for the world
and we stand for the Earth and nature.
And that is something
to get excited about.

Today I Just Wanted To

Today I just wanted to
go outside, look up
at the clouds,
dreaming what it would
be like to reach up
touching God's hand
as He pulled me up
with Him in Heaven
reuniting with Him and Jesus
and my Garry.
Praising God and Jesus
making the impossible possible
worshipping God for eternity,
walking the streets of Heaven
with my Teddy Bear Darling.
It feels so right.
I can't wait for this moment
to be reality,
but in the meantime,
I'll keep trying to
make a difference in this world
through our poetry
and just be me.

Beauty to See

Single walk will do
to see the small things in life
like a bald eagle

soaring above you
or maybe a woodpecker
searching for water.

Open your eyes to
see the beauty in this world
rose opening up

unfolding before
your eyes or a white daisy
What beauty to see!

Elizabeth E. Castillo

Elizabeth Esguerra Castillo

Elizabeth Esguerra Castillo is a multi-awarded and an Internationally-Published Contemporary Author/Poet and a Professional Writer / Creative Writer / Feature Writer / Journalist / Travel Writer from the Philippines. She has 2 published books, "Seasons of Emotions" (UK) and "Inner Reflections of the Muse", (USA). Elizabeth is also a co-author to more than 60 international anthologies in the USA, Canada, UK, Romania, India. She is a Contributing Editor of Inner Child Magazine, USA and an Advisory Board Member of Reflection Magazine, an international literary magazine. She is a member of the American Authors Association (AAA) and PEN International.

Web links:

Facebook Fan Page

https://free.facebook.com/ElizabethEsguerraCastillo

Google Plus

https://plus.google.com/u/0/+ElizabethCastillo

Invisible Hands

The air quivers,
like a harp string touched
by invisible hands.
I hear the silence speak—
a promise wrapped in silver mist,
a horizon that breathes
but never reveals its face.

My heart becomes a vessel,
half-empty, half-brimming,
sailing toward the unknown shore
where time itself waits,
patient as the moon
before it unveils its crown of light.

I stand on the threshold
of a thousand unseen doors,
each key humming in my palm,
and I know—
anticipation is its own kind of magic,
a spell spun from yearning,
woven tighter than fate.

Shadow of the Waters

The river whispers
with the voices of those
who looked back too late.
I drink from its shadowed waters,
taste the salt of what might have been,
and feel the echo of steps
I never dared to take.

The stars, too,
hold their silences like secrets,
burning with truths
I once refused to see.
Every breath I take
is stained with the ash
of abandoned roads.

Yet regret is not only sorrow—
it is a lantern held low,
its flame flickering,
showing me paths unwalked,
teaching me to kneel
before the altar of choices,
and rise again,
even with trembling hands.

Roaring Pride

A mountain lives within me,
crowned with snow,
unyielding to the winds
that gnaw its bones.
I climb its jagged steps,
heart fierce with fire,
eyes bright with the storm.

No voice can bend my spine,
no shadow can tame my blaze.
I wear my victories like constellations,
a robe of suns,
stitched by the gods of daring.

Yet pride is more than thunder—
it is silence after the roar,
the knowing that I stood
where few could stand,
that my breath touched the summit
of impossible skies.
I bow only to the infinite,
for even pride
must kneel before the stars.

Mutawaf Shaheed

Mutawaf Shaheed

C. E. Shy has been writing since the seventh grade. He continued writing through high school, until he became more involved in sports. After his graduation, he worked at the White Motors Company where he wrote for the company's newspaper. He started a column called: "The Poet's Corner." That was his first published work.

www.innerchildpress.com/c-e-shy.php

Bottom Lines

Someone summoned summer, they said they missed
 the butterflies and the rumble of the bumble bees.
They liked the way all the green seems to dominate
the land. They tried their hand at growing some peppers
and other plants. Somebody nicked the picnic bench,
the one at one point helped me survive.

There is an ant walking slowly, boldly across the street
,did he make it across alive? Time for me to sweat again
to get wet again as I run into the rain again. Thunder roars
and lighting strikes definitely play their parts. It's happened
for the last eighty plus years , will it change tonight? I don't
think so.

The sounds change as nature plays an all too familiar tune.
Birds words I hear clearer now, I only wish I knew what
their words mean. Let me get the lawnmower out , this
time I hope it works. I was supposed to paint the picket
fence. First, I must fix the broken gate, Oh, maybe that can
wait. Well since my wife is dead think I'll plant some
flowers
in its stead.

She spent a lot of time tiding up the flower beds. What
should I do with these flower pots? What should I do
with this bass violin, now it seems out of place since all
the music's gone. I know these pots I'll never use. What
to do with the blues I got, I know I'll never lose. The kids
are all gone. I have no idea where the hell they're at.

The honey bees hide in the trees, I'm glad I didn't cut it
down. Since they built the new road there aren't a
lot of passersbys. Spending a little time on line,

unwrapping
other words that don't belong to me. Replacing them with
the ones I write, the ones that keep me free. I spend more
time plugging holes, chasing moles and planning on how to
get them. Never thought things could move so slow.
I sit down faster than I stand.

The distance to the door is still the same, I know I can't blame
that. The floor is a little more intimidating than it was years
before. My friend Byrd, said his every third word is slurred and
did I think he needed to see a shrink? I wrote this song by myself
I can't even say it hurts. Well, the house is tight, so, I just might
change my mind, go outside and jump straight up.

Songs

The song you would sing to me is
still playing, stuck under my thin
skin. I met you during your transition
from awareness; back to the world
of compromise and the living dead.

The things I read the things you said.
I cannot remove. I had no idea then
you were traveling backwards, that
every kiss was saying good-bye.

Every embrace was telling a lie. The
Next time I saw you, you were wearing
a disguise. Your eyes said I still love you.
I guess mine said the same. We both
agreed that life was to blame.

Take A Ways

Searching for the terms that elude me.
Staying away from the places that exclude
me. Smiles that the people cracked, are
now broken by tokens that once thrilled
them. They didn't die laughing. Found
nothing profound in the sounds they made,
the songs they played. Gawking as they
stalk the life of the world, seeking refuge in
soft tissue.

Unaware of the twine wrapped
around their minds, of the wounds left by
nursery rhymes placed there by mother goose.
Never had an accident, always on time for the
appointments that I never made myself. Getting
high on, then overdosing on expectations.
Might be better to want something else.

Reaching for goals with hidden holes. So many
souls got caught in em. Minds anointed with
disappointment then expressing the thoughts
of a dumb cluck. Running in and out of fantasies,
giving charity to cigarettes. Riding the waves with
the malcontents. The subjects of hair brain schemes.

Following the crooked by nature. Had to figure
how to manage the under handed pitches and curve
balls. They been moving the goal post right in front
of my nose. Growing food in delivery trucks while
driving down the streets. Can't completely recover
from the combinations one after another. Even your
home is owned by somebody else , lock, stock and
barrel.

Mutawaf Shaheed

Coming soon to a theater near you, is the latest candidate to show new tricks to you with some new words you have heard before. You stand in line hoping this time they are going be honest with you. Rotten to the core standing at your door, asking you for fifteen cents to watch them straddle the fence then throw you under the bus, to them that makes perfect sense. They have done it so many times before.

There is no shame in the game they play every day. After you select them, they say get outa the way you are messing up my money. Then you go on line and debate, putting your
fate in that blood- sucker's hands. You were crossed out before you put a check in the box by that sold out person's name. I'll close with good luck again, for the two hundred years in a row. Ain't no God anywhere in that flow. I send my condolences to those who lost the war.

hülya n. yılmaz

hülya n. yılmaz

Liberal Arts Professor Emerita, hülya n. yılmaz [sic] is Co-Chair and Director of Editing Services at Inner Child Press International, a published author, ghostwriter, and translator (EN, DE, and TU; in any direction). Her literary contributions appeared in a large number of national and international anthologies.

hülya writes creatively to attain and nourish a comprehensive awareness for and development of our humanity.

hülya n. yılmaz, a traveler on the journey called "life" . . .

Writing Web Site
https://hulyanyilmaz.com/

Editing Web Site
https://hulyasfreelancing.com

A Google Search

Yes, I have . . . asked Google, I mean.
What does "anticipation" mean to the world's experts?
Not a complex or complicated question, right?
Various dictionaries, respected globally, jumped in.
Bear in mind . . . I initiated all of this.

I anticipate a few long hours on the Internet.
Why, I argue against each online entry
As if it were an insult meant only for me.
You see . . . I expect, predict, foresee, foretell,
Prophesize . . . hey, I even forecast an exemplary
Sentence or two.

Busy anticipating a lively argument thanks to Google . . .

what pride?

humanity died

i have stood silently by

my shame has no pride!

regrets

i have always been intrigued
by the well-known last words;
or better yet,
by the final exhales
many avoid calling them "a regret"

however, as we know too well,
no exceptions are allowed
now, soon, or a while later,
each of us will hand over to death
our dear ones, those of our all-encompassing love,
for whom we meant beyond all
that which charades on and on as "life"

could we
in blunt honesty
dissect some facts here?
how many counts, for instance,
show up on our attendance record
when it was *we*,
willing and ready,
stood by during their turn of hardship?

how many times, if ever at all,
have we gifted them with the core of our soul?

that they are gone
barges into our minds
we breathe anew our unsettled doubts,
adeptly disguised as regrets

oh, those regrets!
they fatally define
the remainder of our time

because
neither life of their molding for our sakes
nor Earth which they served to us as a world divine,
or the many a ground they spread out for us in devotion
to make bearable the blow of our most wearisome treks
is anymore

thus, we get swept away,
simply farther and farther away
from what once seemed to be an indestructible fort
into the raging squalls of a maddest river
that sprints to ally with its wild sea
with no mercy

and

thus, we get continually overthrown
by the smallest undertows of our years

somehow we still manage
to stay afloat long enough
to ask them for their forgiveness
in eternal absentia

in our final moment, however,
we might by a wild chance remember:
time does not wait for any of us
we cannot say: "i am sorry"

in the final moment, however,
we might by a wild chance remember:
there will be no grace period anymore
if at all, time will be there for a blink of the eye

all along, we will be planning to meet
our often-envisioned deadline,
the one that will be bridging our two vital breaths:
the privileged first and the barely audible last

* *"Regrets" (modified here) is an old poem dear to my heart.*

Teresa E. Gallion

Teresa E. Gallion

Teresa E. Gallion is a seeker on a journey to work on unfolding spiritually in this present lifetime. Writing is a spiritual exercise for Teresa. Her passions are traveling the world and hiking the mountain and desert landscapes of the western United States. Her journeys into nature are nurtured by the Sufi poets Rumi and Hafiz. The land is sacred ground and her spiritual temple where she goes for quiet reflection and contemplation. She has published five books: Walking Sacred Ground, Contemplation in the High Desert, Chasing Light, a finalist in the 2013 New Mexico/Arizona Book Awards, Scent of Love, a finalist in the 2021 New Mexico/Arizona Book Awards and Come Egypt in 2024. She has two CDs, *On the Wings of the Wind* and *Poems from Chasing Light*. Her work has appeared in numerous journals and anthologies.

Website: http://teresagallion.yolasite.com/

Anticipatory Desire

The wind holds a conference before it speaks.
Patience waits for the breeze
to carry the message that floats gently
on the airwaves of time and space.

Each whisper in the wind
pulls on the heart strings
like rainbows on a free ride.
The breeze is anticipated

like a new lover coming to visit.
Hold your breath after a long inhale.
Footsteps freeze below the clouds.
The universe speaks with authority.

What will the message be
on a slow riding day?
Let it be the friend of hope
with blessings for a desperate soul.

Pathway of Regret

The trail calls me into the pines.
No guidance or suggestions
on the route to pursue.
It is a crapshoot of potential regret.

Choices are made daily.
Some boil over and burn the feet.
The dark shadows hang like heavy burdens.
Only chaos stirs the brain.

You wander in the ashes
of the pathway made.
Feel the cold birth of hard choices
and the realization of the value of regret.

That is when you recognize
regret is the path to new beginnings.
The lessons learned build strong bones.
Spiritual fire warms the soul.

Jemez Red Rock Moment

A blade of grass bows to the wind.
The breeze says hello beautiful.
My eyes lock on a light wave
running across a red rock sentinel.

The clouds hang low
like a fluffy blanket atop the wall.
Gives me a love hug and splatters my brain
across sacred red pueblo sand.

I lay against a juniper branch.
It sings growth into my reshaped brainwaves.
Another break-through in my Spiritual evolution.

The solitude overwhelms me with joy.
The smile on my face is radiant.
Giant little reddish-brown lizards
race in the sand close to my footprints.

Ashok K. Bhargava

Ashok K. Bhargava

Ashok Bhargava is a poet, writer, inspirational speaker and a literary consultant. He has attended poetry conferences in Italy, Turkey, India and Philippines. His latest book "Riding the Tide" about his battle with cancer has been translated and published in Arabic, Hindi, Telugu and Bengali languages. He is a contributing writer to several anthologies worldwide including World Poetry Almanac 2014. He has been published in numerous print and online magazines.

Ashok has won many accolades including Poet Ambassador to Japan, Kalidasa International award, World Poetry Lifetime Achievement award, Writers Beyond Borders Peace award and Tapsilog Leadership award for his community involvement. He is founder of Writers International Network Canada Society to discover, nourish, recognize and celebrate writers, poets and artists and to assist them to network with the community at large. He is the author of eight books of poetry and one anthology. He is Artist-in-Residence at Moberly Arts & Cultural Centre and also co-edits the literary section of The Link Newspaper.

Quiet Regret

We walked away —
fuming,
shouting.
Not peaceful.

One last attempt
to patch the cracks
had already crumbled
beneath us.

There were still words
waiting in our mouths,
but they had lost their weight.
We both knew.

We had tried —
as much as we knew how.
So we stepped back,
trying to cool it,

to stop the unraveling,
as if space between us
might somehow
hold us together.

Outside,
a few streaks of light
still hung from the sunset.
We regretted, probably —

not just what was said,
but what we didn't say.

Quiet regret
settled around us.

The sky —
a scatter of stars
and something like forgiveness —
waited overhead,

so full
of sparkling love
and hope.

If only
we had looked up.

The Long Silence

Most likely, you'll still be here
when we are gone —
and somehow,
that comforts us:
that something of us
will continue
through you.

Life moves in one direction—
no returning,
no second meetings
here or elsewhere.

But that's not tragic.
It's natural.
Everything that exists
leans toward its ending.

What matters
are the moments—
how we breathe them,
share them,
let them shape us.

Life is one long moment,
stitched from many small ones.

Knowing how to live it
is fragile—
always slipping.

Still,
you carry part of us.
Like the gift we gave you
that snowy March evening—
earned in sweat,
filled with love,
meant simply:
we wanted to be close to you.

Misunderstanding
dried it into a scab.

It will fall.
Don't worry.

Even our pain
belongs
to eternity.

Anticipation of New Dawn

There is no silence
we cannot outwait—
even stone leans in to hear the coming light.

There is no fury
we cannot cool—
though its embers glow beneath the surface.

Dawn lingers like a flag of truce
held in trembling hands,
or the stillness before old ghosts march.

It might be the breath of a newborn,
or pride readying its war cry.

God may be a lighthouse,
or a mirror catching shadows.

Light, a blade yet to be drawn;
shadow, a veil yet to be lifted.

We stand at the threshold,
scarred by our own longing—

Will we heal, or harden?
Will we rise from ash,
or wait beneath the flame?

Caroline 'Ceri Naz' Nazareno Gabis

Caroline 'Ceri' Nazareno-Gabis

Caroline 'Ceri Naz' Nazareno-Gabis, author of Velvet Passions of Calibrated Quarks, World Poetry Canada International Director to Philippines is a multi-awarded poet, editor, journalist, educator, peace and women's advocate. She believes that learning other's language and culture is a doorway to wisdom.

Among her poetic belts include **Gabrielle Galloni Memorial Panorama International Youth Award** 2022, Panorama Youth Literary Awards 2020, 7th Prize Winner in the 19th, 20th and 21st Italian Award of Literary Festival; Writers International Network-Canada ''Amazing Poet 2015'', The Frang Bardhi Literary Prize 2014 (Albania), Poet Journalist Award 2014 (Tuzla, Istanbul, Turkey) and World Poetry Empowered Poet 2013 (Vancouver, Canada). She's a featured member of Association of Women's Rights and Development (AWID), The Poetry Posse, Galaktika Poetike, Asia Pacific Writers and Translators (APWT), Axlepino and Anacbanua. Her poetry and children's stories have been featured in different anthologies and magazines worldwide.

Links to her works:

http://panitikan.ph/2018/03/30/caroline-nazareno-gabis/

https://apwriters.org/author/ceri_naz/

http://www.aveviajera.org/nacionesunidasdelasletras/id1181.html

Tomorrow's Promise

Everytime I lean on the windowpane,
I can see a silent vow somehow,
The moonlight spills a suspended world,
A silver hope,
A warm breath,
A calming pause,
The stars hear my wishes,
Beyond the heartbeat and soft refrains,
Each heartbeat hums a song of praise,
Each refrain writes a morning light,
I rise with my cups filled with courage,
A sacred space and a hush of dawn,
The time embraces the passionate pearl,
Where windows of dreams take root into your eyes.

The Weight of a Missed Chance

I have a visitor.
It has no face,
It is a shadow of words I screamed,
It is the feeling I told you before,
It is the happiness I have not shown,
It is a touch of a reminder,
It is the change I long to hear.
It whispers, what was the story?
If only I could tell, how much
I desired, as I want, and as I loved
To retract a memory lane
To exchange a missed chance
Of a maybe and what if
To what I should have now,
Today, I sit and regret,
Looking for another chance.

The Highest Hill He Chose

Alone, he planted his stubborn feet
To the highest hill he always wanted,
The wind warned him,
To be gentler, to be kinder,
Go to the soft ground,
Move a little slow
But seem to be so sure
About this hill,
Unknown that the pain is coming,
Up the hill, the highest climb,
Never anticipated what lies ahead,
Where too much ego
 is louder than a big fall.

Swapna Behera

Swapna Behera

Swapna Behera is a trilingual poet, translator, environmentalist, editor from India and author of seven books of different genres including one on children's literature on Environment. She is the recipient of International UGADI AWARD 2019, honoured from Gujurat Sahitya Akademi 2022, 2021 International Poesis Award of Honor as Jury, Pentasi B World Fellow Poet, Honoured Poet of India from Seychelles Government and International awards from Algeria, Morocco, Kajhakhstan, modern Arabic Literary Renaissance of Egypt, International Arts Council Argentina etc. Her stories, poems, articles are published in many International and National magazines and ezines. Her poem A NIGHT IN THE REFUGEE CAMP is translated into 67 languages. She has received over 60 National and International Awards. At present she is the Cultural Ambassador for India and South Asia of Inner Child and the life member of Odisha Environmental Society

Email
swapna.behera@gmail.com

Web Site
http://swapnabehera.in/

anticipation
(anticipation is an emotion – Robert Plutchik)

perfidious dreams
a visual narrative
moth's metamorphic journey
to be a butterfly

hope mingled with trust
melodies of indelible memories
magical folklore
traditional chivalry
or
Buddhist theory of emotions
that roots to lot of experience of the past
leading to a canopy of future
anticipations are polar stars
visions to live and die for tomorrow

regret of the seminars

intellectuals with their voluminous files
present in the round table seminars
their agendas cleanly enclosed
with soft and hard copies
sophisticated five-star snacks
chefs alert, delegates with their personal secretaries, media
all ready
to discuss food security
farmers issues, more productive land
but where is the farmer delegate?
he has to speak volumes
fertility is lost
scarcity of rain
unpredictable climate
he is the ground worker
who tills land, guards the crops
takes them to the local market
sells them to the capitalist brokers in cheap rate
at times leave them in the land itself
too cheap is the harvest
the logistic cost is higher than the cost of production
too tough to handle policy files
poor farmer is trapped
in the loop of fractured democracy
soldiers in the war field
refugees with orphans
can someone ever define regret?

pride, prejudice and self-esteem

pride is a scarecrow
sitting in the middle of the brain
with a self-made paper crown on the head
for its imaginary empire
just a shadow
having no diameter
the mirage
the thematic stone statue
I, ME, MYSELF create the ego zone
where there is no place for humanity
or pragmatic solution
birds can sit on the scarecrow
 and sing a song of the sky
they can fly and create their zone
The Sun and rain tear up the scare crow
it melts in the soil to be the fertilizer
pride is a basket of eggs on the head
the lonely narcist's slogan
a dust cauldron
near the sea shore

prejudice is the tortoise in the traffic
the conglomeration
the prodigal son returning to his father
when the heart is on the microphone

ask the granny the definition of self esteem
a do or die slogan
Gen z of all land
a fight within
for liberty, equality and fraternity
no sugarcoating words
no fermentation, no isms
only a big full stop for all corruption

Albert 'Infinite' Carrasco

Albert 'Infinite' Carassco

Albert "Infinite The Poet" Carrasco is an urban poet, mentor and public speaker.

Albert believes his experience of growing up in poverty, dealing with drugs and witnessing murder over and over were lessons learnt, in order to gain knowledge to teach. Albert's harsh reality and honesty is a powerfully packed punch delivered through rhyme. Infinite grew up in the east part of the Bronx and still resides there, so he knows many young men will follow the same dark path he followed looking for change. The life of crime should never be an option to being poor but it is, very often.

Infinite poetry @lulu.com

Alcarrasco2 on YouTube

Infinite the poet on reverbnation

Infinite Poetry

www.lulu.com/us/en/shop/al-infinite-carrasco/infinite-poetry/paperback/product-21040240.html

www.innerchildpress.com/albert-carrasco

Anticipation regret pride

When I was young I watched my mother struggle to make ends meet, she was super woman to my brothers and i. She was always on her feet hustling to pay bills and to make sure there was something for us to eat. I admired her strength to cope, she was a single parent due to her losing her life partner, my father, to cancer. I was getting older and just watching her struggle was something that couldn't be done any longer. I was going to help her. As her son, that was my anticipation.

As a young boy I chased the root of all evil to bring us joy. There was nothing scarier than being a minor in a game for adult players, I wasn't going to look back, I was going to rise up and be a respected hustler in the trap. It took some time but I did just that. I'm pushing rocked up grams with friends I played with in the sand, we weren't poor anymore, we could dig in our pockets at anytime and pull out a few grand. We're living life to the fullest and yet to have any regrets.

In the upcoming years a plague spread murder as it was a disease, I prayed for the best but yet the worst was conceived, there's nothing but air around us but a lot of my friends died because they couldn't breathe, they were gasping for air begging the lord please as they was running out of breath due to acts of soul thieves. I should've left, I saw an exit out the trap but I stood inside, I continued to ride, at that time I couldn't walk away from what I started before the dearly departed, because of pride.

Kimberly Burnham

Kimberly Burnham

A brain health expert (PhD in Integrative Medicine) and award-winning poet, Kimberly Burnham lives with her wife and family in Spokane, Washington. Kim speaks extensively on peace, brain health, and "*Awakenings: Peace Dictionary, Language and the Mind, a Daily Brain Health Program.*" She recently published "*Heschel and King Marching to Montgomery A Jewish Guide to Judeo-Tamarian Imagery.*" Currently work includes "*Call and Response To Maya Stein an Anthology of Wild Writing"* and a how-to non-fiction book, "*Using Ekphrastic Fiction Writing and Poetry to Create Interest and Promote Artists, Writers, and Poets.*"

Follow her at https://amzn.to/4fcWnRB

The Heart Holding Tight

Hope is more than waiting
the Spanish word "Esperar" means to wait and to hope
more significance still
in Tepeuxila Cuicatec, a language of Mexico
hope is called "wait-desire"
a blend of two activities

In Ngäbere of Costa Rica the phrase for hope
"resting the mind" implies waiting and confidence
hope is confident waiting

In the Indonesian language Mairasi
hope is translated vision resting place
as if we have to see something in our mind's eye
before we can hope for it

Noongar speakers of Guyana say "Koort-kwidiny" means heart waiting
where "Coer nagal nyjininyj Ngulla Boodja"
translated "may peace prevail on earth"
literally means "we are sitting together on our country"

In Marathi of India hope "Aasha" (आशा) with a stronger emphasis on desire
while in Tamil "Nampikkai" (நம்பிக்கை) with a stronger emphasis on expectation
hope in Adyghe of North-west Caucasus Russia "the heart expects something good"
the African language of Keliko "place one's heart on the head"
and in Somrai of Chad hope is "hold the heart really tight"
as if our heart has to sit confidently and see
and hold tight to hope for peace

A Rainbow of Hope

In Anjam hope is "looking through the horizon"
in the mountainous land of Papua New Guinea
while in a neighboring language, Dobu "Nuwaila" is to think back
the next word in the dictionary is "Nuwaiyai" means to hope
then "Nuwa'i'isi" is to remember and "Nuwa'ila is retrospection
and a sign of hope for better weather ahead "Ulele" is a rainbow

While half a world away in Tanzania's Mwera
"hope" and "faith" are translated with the same word "Ngulupai"
where "Kupingana" is love and "Ulele" peace

In Nigeria's Berom hope is translated "direct one's liver toward"
as if it is not only our mind where we hope but in our body
in our liver and heart
while in Mixtepec Mixtec of Mexico hope
is "wait and remain strong on the inside"

Tswana speakers of South Africa say "Tsholofelo"
"hope, expect, look for confidently"
while Uganda's Luganda "Okusuubira" means "hope, trust and expect"
also "look forward to, rely upon, anticipate, reckon"
as if hope is something that can't be done alone but only with trust
in someone or something and with someone to rely on

Shir Tikvah Song of Hope

In Hebrew שיר תקווה [Shir Tikvah] means song of hope
Tikvah (תִּקְוָה) or hope comes from the root "Kavah" (קָוָה)
implying "gathering, binding or waiting with expectation"
also the literal sense of a cord or rope
something tangible to grasp
we hold on in the face of such sadness and despair in the world
"Tikvah" symbolizes the strong, enduring, and faithful
expectation of a better future
central to Jewish culture
as we sing HaTikvah (הַתִּקְוָה) or "The Hope"
and shine a light where there is darkness
while we remember that we are all connected

Eliza Segiet

Eliza Segiet

Eliza Segiet graduated with a Master's Degree in Philosophy at Jagiellonian University.

Received *Global Literature Guardian Award* – from Motivational Strips, World Nations Writers Union and Union Hispanomundial De Escritores (UHE) 2018.

Nominated for the Pushcart Prize 2019, 2021.

Laureate *Naji Naaman Literary Prize 2020*,

International Award Paragon of Hope (2020),

World Award 2020 *Cesar Vallejo* for Literary Excellence. Laureate of the Special Jury *Sahitto International Award* 2021, World Award *Premiul Fănuș Neagu* 2021.

Finalist *Golden Aster Book* World Literary Prize 2020, *Mili Dueli* 2022, Voci nel deserto 2022.

At the international Festival of Poetry CAMPIONATO MONDIALE DI POESIA (2021/2022) she won the title of vice-champion of the world.

Award BHARAT RATNA RABINDRANATH TAGORE INTERNATIONAL AWARD (2022).

Award - *World Poets Association* (2023).

Laureate Between words and infinity *"International Literary Award (2023)*.

Eliza Segiet

Snowdrops

It seemed impossible,
yet it happened once again!
She looked at her
while she was asleep, astonished.
Many-colored needles adorned her body,
saving her life, intending to wake her up.
In the embrace of uncertainty,
the friend waited impatiently
for her to wake up.
She whispered to her, but
all she heard was the sound
of the respirator breaking the silence.

Anxiety, anticipation, hope –
this made it possible to believe
that a miracle could happen.
Though the doctor said:
– *This is the final ward!*

Against all expectations,
a slow awakening began.
A return to the world,
where machines
would become only a memory.

The strings of reality
were badly frayed,
her memory was returning slowly.
Yet, the joy
that she had managed to come back
whitened like a field
strewn with snowdrops.

Translated by Dorota Stępińska

Choices

His life
was torn by relentless regrets.
So many opportunities he could have seized,
yet he made so many wrong decisions.
It could have been different –
beautiful, maybe even rich!
There could have been fortune,
yet all that's left is the frustration and sorrow.

All choices
have a date of expiry.
After that, they go off.

Translated by Dorota Stępińska

Moon Dust

No one believed in him
"He won't make it."
He took it as his fate,
and stopped even trying
to do anything.

But on one sunny
September day,
like in a one-horse chariot,
he began to move
towards the fulfilment of his dreams.

He made it!
He felt as though he were
surrounded by the moon dust,
illuminated by the sun
and, most importantly –
by wisdom.

He didn't allow himself
to get lost in prophecies,
he immersed himself in the dance of the future.
He knew that
to succeed –
was to believe in himself.

Translated by Dorota Stępińska

William S. Peters Sr.

William S. Peters, Sr.

Bill's writing career spans a period of well over 50 years. Being first Published in 1972, Bill has since went on to Author in excess of 50+ additional Volumes of Poetry, Short Stories, etc., expressing his thoughts on matters of the Heart, Spirit, Consciousness and Humanity. His primary focus is that of Love, Peace and Understanding!

Bill says . . .

I have always likened Life to that of a Garden. So, for me, Life is simply about the Seeds we Sow and Nourish. All things we "Think and Do", will "Be" Cause and eventually manifest itself to being an "Effect" within our own personal "Existences" and "Experiences" . . . whether it be Fruit, Flowers, Weeds or Barren Landscapes! Bill highly regards the Fruits of his Labor and wishes that everyone would thus go on to plant "Lovely" Seeds on "Good Ground" in their own Gardens of Life!

to connect with Bill, he is all things Inner Child

www.iaminnerchild.com

Personal Web Site

www.iamjustbill.com

Anticipation, Regret and Pride
To Dream

I looked forward towards what was to come.

Ignoring what was,

But I had no regrets,

For my pride could not admit

This weakness I had

To dream

Re-Fractal

Refractal reflections
Of a life gone by
And we humans oft ask
The question 'why'

Patch-quilt dreams
Of hopes to come
Neglectful we are
Of our holy sum

We Were created to conquer
Yet we oft times lie
In await for an end
Where we believe we die

We are strong and powerful
But we only suspect
Our Soul's potential
Awoken not yet

As time goes by
And its illusions embraced
Truth is a fear
Rarely by us faced

But somewhere deeply buried
In the soul of us all
Is a power and knowing
Awaiting our call

Nowhere is it written
That we were born to accept
This maleable fate
That is quite suspect

William S. Peters, Sr.

Let us gather ourselves people
And press ourselves forward
For this novel we now write
Is only the fore-word

Telling of content
Yet to unfold
When we fulfill the promises
Spoken of old

I believe soon come the day
When we open our eyes
And the truth of our divinity
Will be fully realized

Re-Fractal

We Old Folk

The aches and the pains
And the challenge of balance
Are but a few of the things
We must endure

We still like good food,
But yet again comes a challenge
For we never know
What good food will do

Those afternoon naps
Are quite heavenly
I wished I had discovered them before
To be rested yet tired
No longer fired up
To go running through any doors

Forgetful memories for
Car keys and glasses
And reasons I go room to room
Still yet I dream of my younger days
When I lived like a blaze
With no cares about things of doom

My thoughts here to there
And back again
I can't remember my old friend's name.
I find myself
Wasting much time
On devices playing games

My hair changing color
Falling out or going away
Oh did I mention the aches and pains?
Day after day

The same routines
With anxieties coming to play

I think of my children
And what is to come
For they are the sum of me
And as days go by
I ask myself why
Do things have to be what they be

We old folk still wonder
What is to come of our world
And the plight of humanity's ways
Oh, just a thought I play with
At times as time goes by
Seeking to peacefully live out each day

We Old Folk

October 2025 Featured Poets

Фросина Тасевска

Tanja Ajtic

Jerome L. Duque

Priyanka Neogi

Фросина Тасевска

Фросина Тасевска

Фросина Тасевска aka Frosina Tasevska was born in Shtip, the Republic of Macedonia. She is a bilingual poet and writer who creates in both English and Macedonian. Passionate about words since an early age, she has authored two solo poetry collections and continues to work on new manuscripts. Her writings have been published in numerous national and international magazines, newspapers, and anthologies, where her voice is recognized for its depth and emotional resonance. She is an active member of various literary platforms and has received several awards for her creative work, honoring her contribution to contemporary poetry.

Molten Wildflowers

I was not merely planted —
I was forged by fire.
The flames didn't seek permission.
They surged through,
devouring every tender root
I believed it made me whole.
Ash became my foundation,
Smoke, my sky.
And yet—
Something deep within me
Refused to perish.
From bone and ember,
Petals emerged.
Cracked open by heat,
Softness still broke through.
I did not bloom despite the flames—
I bloomed because of them.
A wildflower crafted, not found.
Molten, and still alive.

Something More

I am something more
than a song with underlined words,
more than overwhelming silences,
more than burning warmth.
More than a sleepy smile,
a peculiarity in the depth of breath.
More than your sunrise
and my sunset,
more than a gentle, tight embrace.
I am something more
than a spark from heated pupils,
more than a hazy dream,
more than the fiery blaze
that runs from the peak of the lips,
more than a thought thrown into oblivion.
I am something,
something more than memories
stretching into infinity.
I am more love than affection.

What if?

What if you followed the path your heart desires?
What if you broke free from the chains of fear
and embraced your true self?
What if others judge you, but you respond with a smile?

What if you chose silence over empty words,
remaining composed when they don't understand,
and listening to the powerful voice within you?
What if you embraced joy and cultivated peace?
What if you stumbled but rose stronger than before,
if you shed tears yet never lost hope,
and continued to walk with your head held high?
What if you were different, unique, and unyielding?
What if you decided to prioritize loving yourself
over seeking approval, to be the best friend to your soul
and nurture the light that shines within you?
What if the ultimate freedom is simply being yourself
and not being swayed by the opinions of others?

Life is yours; your strength belongs to you.
Write your own story with unwavering courage.
Let the world have its say, while you choose to live!

Tanja Ajtic

Tanja Ajtic

Tanja Ajtic was born in Belgrade. Since 2002 she lives in Canada. In 2023 she returned to Belgrade. She is a member of many groups. Her poems and stories have been published in more than two hundred collections, anthologies and electronic books. Her poems have been published in fifteen world languages. She published a book of poetry "Outlines of Love". She won the "Cita Del Galateo" Antonio De Ferrariis, 2022" - Rome; the 2023 literary award of the "Naji Naaman" Foundation from the Republic of Lebanon, as well as many other prestigious awards. She writes poetry, short stories ect.

A River

You who live near the river
You believe in images of little gods of love
in ancient Roman art
and Renaissance as well as a new era.
In a lovely little winged children entertained with
various jobs
you see them and speak like Socrates:
"I know I do not know anything!".
You say that the world is a property without a master
and that it is not known who its creator is?
You as a free thinker, neither good nor bad,
indifferent, but not powerless.
You see those beautiful children in the glare of the river
which flows for you into infinity and you enjoy.
You have a safe haven and enough air
to survive everything
in the air that can cause it
chemical changes and you can calculate them
only if you want.
You live in your own reflection of an image
and I believe you
that the world can be a nice place
if we look at ourselves.
Then everything is clear.

Eternal Curse

We like to emphasize splendor, significance, reputation and fame
rather than modesty, contrition and true love.
We want to give one thing a relief that catches the eye,
to be particulary emphasized.
And if we have relief maps, we don't know how to measure.
We wander and saunter at night.
At night without dreams.
We postpone forgiveness and omissions.
We are postponing our payment deadline,
we also want to have a discount while we are paying,
and we would like to do everything to make it cheaper.
And paradise is not bought but deserved.
If we return everything we took
and wish forgiveness of sins, mercy and forgiveness,
to be forgiven we will feel the same.
After the main flowering, the flowers will bloom once again.
And we will survive.
Like being born again
the revival of classical antiquity
or more precisely freedom
and the creative human spirit under the influence of classical literature,
of art and philosophy in the Renaissance.
We will renew our lives
and fix and change it for the better.
We will refresh and rejuvenate.
We will look at hummingbirds that have bigger brain
in relation to the body of other birds.
Heart too.
These birds can fly

in all directions, as they please!
They can live for a long time by feeding on
flower nectar and candied water.
We, like them, are small but a lot is expected of us.
Rejection and refusal,
as a musical repetition of the same tone, the
opposite is an echo.
Everything will resonate.
Rejection and refusal happen to us
like breaks in a circus that clowns fill with their jokes.
We avoid the eternal curse
because there is always hope for a corrective exam
and a place under the sun for us.
We can be dignified,
be those who produce again,
which recreate.
We can multiply and experience
content to revive consciousness,
get a good voice again
for the person and respect, reputation and name.
It is never too late for natural things
to make us feel better.
It's all in us
in our big hearts in the body of a small hummingbird.
We have everything you need!
Naturally!

Passion

The water of your body
flowed into mine
in ecstasy,
and the universe drew nearer
that night.
While our sighs
rose into cries,
filling
the space
of the room, the bed,
and the tangled sheets
with the scent of lilacs
and the dampness,
the fragrance of spring rain.
Through a cry
I spoke your
name,
murmuring of love,
of passion,
in the timeless space
of love.
I was filled
with our passion,
with the celestial music
of eternal union,
of the primordial beginning.

Jerome L. Duque

Jerome L. Duque

Jerome L. Duque is a Filipino dreamer exploring the universes of words: as a writer, creating them; as an educator, shaping them in young scribes; and as a chronicler, ensuring that they are etched on paper. When not working, he's usually plotting his next adventures elsewhere in the Milky Way.

Bucolic

Crickets chirping in the morning grass;
Then, dawn chorus of tree sparrows.
A cold zephyr rustling the bamboo leaves,
Dewdrops plopping on puddles–
Sounds that break the silence
Of a forgotten country–
As I retire
From clatter of keys,
Revving engines on a rush hour,
Staccato of office chatter,
And erupting squeals of black boxes.

My blood sings for a slow daybreak,
As I languor in bed,
Thinking of the pots I'm filling
And the blossoms I'm picking.

Cusp

I would've made the jump
Over the cliff,
Not minding the depth
Nor the crimps. I may never reach.

I could've just dove
Into the torrent that runs through the gorge
Without the certainty
Of ever ending up at the bay.

I should've just leapt,
Even without wings,
With only the courage to dare
The limits of life and fate.

But I didn't,
So I must, again, wait.

Versus

A man has two faces:
One smiles;
the other grins.
The first holds his head high,
While someone looks down his fellow's nose
A stout heart he has,
Another's just a hollow.
This doesn't fly too close to the sun
That turns to ashes.
Faces, or masks?
To wear, to keep, to live with.
Two, but also one.

Priyanka Neogi

Priyamka Neogi

Amb. Dr. Priyanka Neogi born is 2.7.1988 at Coochbehar, India. She is a professional librarian, was government school teacher, business women, Honorary doctorate from Theophany University of Haiti. She is an international poet, International story writer, lecturer, Author, translator, International columnist, Essayist, photographer, International Live telecaster, host, cultural enthusiast, Educator, Keynote Speaker, Researcher, Kathak dancer, Rabindra Dancer, Folk Dancer, song, wheelschel, Artist, short drama. Performer, Judge, Acting, International reciter, International motivational speaker, Country Director, Journalist, N.S.S, computer course of Cita & tally, literacy organisational of national and international. She is multi-talented and awardee of multi-purpose.

I'm Your Love Bird,

I'm your dance,
singing version,
rhythm of recitation,
tune of guitar,
scale of piano,
therapy of nature.
your heart sings for me,
I'm your crash,
your moment makes me flash.

I'm your dream & sunshine,
make you brighter.
I'm your sea,
super power feel the story,
I'm your mountain & sky,
 feel me high.

You're glad about me,
love smell allows you,
caring nature attracts me.

I'm your love bird,
makes you passionate,
I'm your happiness,
 create a lovely time.
I'm your Miss universe & miss world,
as a supportive person always behind.
day by day it makes you stronger.
Feeling mind fresh when talking with me,
you are always interested in me.

I m your heart bird mental peace of your life,
create a dream after getting meetings,

my love network gives you,
love-line of love.

I m your love bird,
courage to everything.
When we are travelling weather give us amazing
colour,
every time make new story of love,
You know how beautiful the perfect one.

I should be a lover

Flower basket in flower garden,
Mind-blowing visionary,
Life guard of drifting,
Rules and regulations.

Lover your life is in the tide,
Continue story sky the yolk
Sweet harmony in the union of hearts,
I Think stretch is a colorful dawn.

Lover is your companion in happiness and sorrow,
Tears are forgotten and a unique smile appears on the lips.
Reluctance to seek the warmth of a relationship,
Sweet words bring perfection to the mind.

In the mind of a lover as a lover,
As the ever-present spring,
Build a sky of exuberance,
Let me be in the ocean of love.

I will be your bride one day.
betel leaf betel nut tip on the forehead,
Surroundings illuminated with love.
Be your lover according to my love rules,
I will decorate my life with you.

Lock of Heart with Heart,

Flowers fall from trees.
the flowers are stuck,
As long as the tree holds the flower,
Or as long as flowers want to last,
Set with trees.

The bond of love between two people,
Mind colored pulse,
Both intent on holding each other,
Talk about what is in the heart.
Locking heart with heart,
Happiness is the companion of sorrow,
Move forward for each other.

In the third person tense,
Let the foreigner burn,
block the other.
Do not enter into the enclosure of the mind.
In the dirty obsession of mind,
to color the mind,
I will pour spring.

Locking heart with his heart,
Keep the key to yourself.
Abyssal guards at the border of love,
Don't let anyone in.
With love and affection,
Keeping the mind fresh with the mind,
It will be a happy and colorful life.

Remembering

our fallen soldiers of verse

Janet Perkins Caldwell
February 14, 1959 ~ September 20, 2016

Alan W. Jankowski
16 March 1961 ~ 10 March 2017

Shareef Abdur Rasheed
30 May 1945 ~ 11 February 2025

The Butterfly Effect

"IS" in effect

Inner Child Press

News

Published Books
by
Poetry Posse Members

We are so excited to share and announce a few of the current books, as well as the new and upcoming books of some of our Poetry Posse authors.

On the following pages we present to you ...

Alicja Maria Kuberska

Jackie Davis Allen

Gail Weston Shazor

hülya n. yılmaz

Nizar Sartawi

Elizabeth E. Castillo

Faleeha Hassan

Fahredin Shehu

Kimberly Burnham

Caroline 'Ceri' Nazareno

Eliza Segiet

Teresa E. Gallion

Mutawaf Shaheed

William S. Peters, Sr.

Now Available
www.innerchildpress.com

The Year of the Poet XII October 2025

KREW ŻYCIA

The Blood of Life

Eliza Segiet

Translated by Dorota Stępińska

Now Available
www.innerchildpress.com

Now Available

The Year of the Poet XII October 2025

www.innerchildpress.com

Bir Zamanlar Türkiye'de

hülya n. yılmaz

Now Available

Inner Child Press News

www.innerchildpress.com

Now Available

The Year of the Poet XII October 2025

www.innerchildpress.com

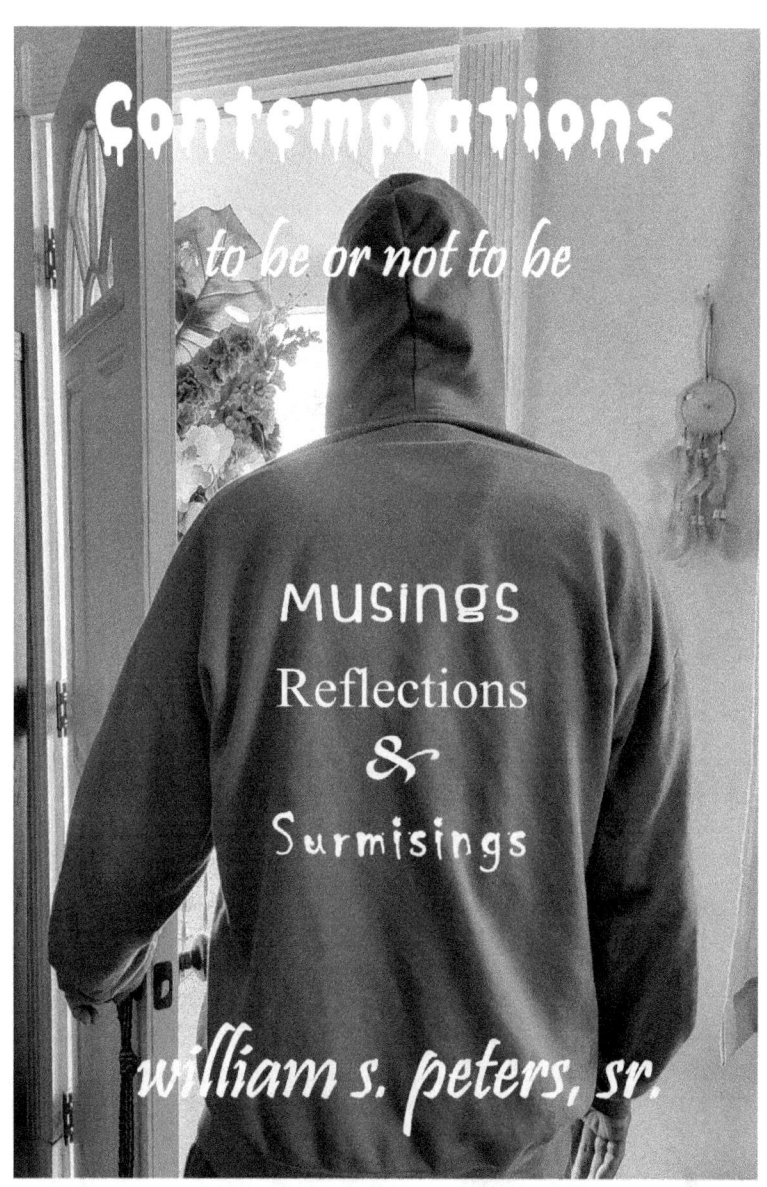

Inner Child Press News

Now Available

www.innerchildpress.com

The Year of the Poet XII October 2025

Now Available
www.innerchildpress.com

Inner Child Press News

Now Available
www.innerchildpress.com

Now Available
www.innerchildpress.com

Inner Child Press News

Now Available
www.innerchildpress.com

The Year of the Poet XII October 2025

Now Available
www.innerchildpress.com

Inner Child Press News

Now Available
www.innerchildpress.com

The Year of the Poet XII October 2025

Now Available
www.innerchildpress.com

Inner Child Press News

Now Available
www.innerchildpress.com

The Year of the Poet XII October 2025

Now Available at
www.innerchildpress.com

Inner Child Press News

Now Available at
www.amazon.com/gp/product/B08MYL5B7S/ref=
dbs_a_def_rwt_hsch_vapi_tkin_p1_i2

The Year of the Poet XII October 2025

Now Available
www.innerchildpress.com

Inner Child Press News

Now Available
www.innerchildpress.com

The Year of the Poet XII October 2025

Now Available
www.innerchildpress.com

Inner Child Press News

Now Available
www.innerchildpress.com

The Year of the Poet XII October 2025

Inner Child Press News

Now Available
www.innerchildpress.com

Now Available
www.innerchildpress.com

Inner Child Press News

Now Available
www.innerchildpress.com

The Year of the Poet XII October 2025

Now Available
www.innerchildpress.com

Inner Child Press News

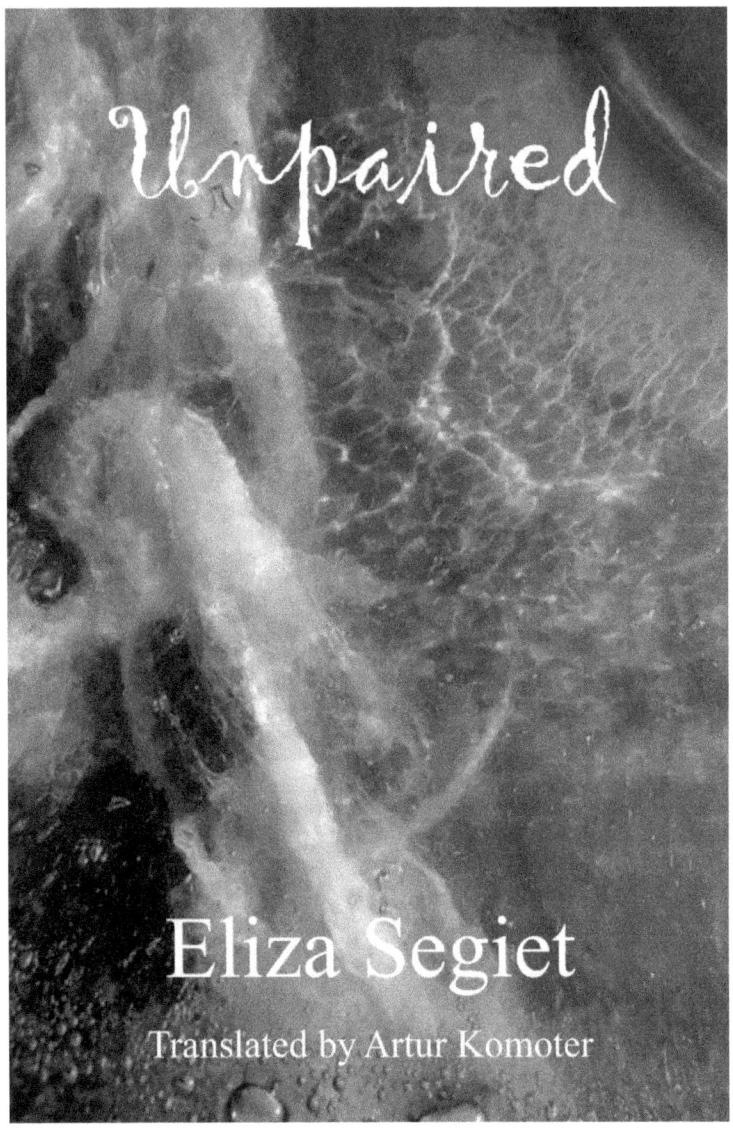

Now Available
www.innerchildpress.com

The Year of the Poet XII October 2025

Private Issue
www.innerchildpress.com

Inner Child Press News

Now Available at
www.innerchildpress.com

The Year of the Poet XII October 2025

Now Available at
www.innerchildpress.com

Inner Child Press News

Now Available at
www.innerchildpress.com

The Year of the Poet XII October 2025

Now Available at
www.innerchildpress.com

Inner Child Press News

HERENOW

FAHREDIN SHEHU

Now Available at
www.innerchildpress.com

The Year of the Poet XII October 2025

Now Available at
www.innerchildpress.com

Now Available at
www.innerchildpress.com

The Year of the Poet XII October 2025

Now Available at
www.innerchildpress.com

Inner Child Press News

Now Available at
www.innerchildpress.com

The Year of the Poet XII October 2025

Now Available at
www.innerchildpress.com

Inner Child Press News

Breakfast
for
Butterflies

Faleeha Hassan

Now Available at
www.innerchildpress.com

The Year of the Poet XII October 2025

Now Available at
www.innerchildpress.com

Now Available at
www.innerchildpress.com

The Year of the Poet XII October 2025

Now Available at
www.innerchildpress.com

Now Available at
www.innerchildpress.com

The Year of the Poet XII October 2025

Now Available
www.innerchildpress.com

Other Anthological works from

Inner Child Press International

www.innerchildpress.com

Inner Child Press Anthologies

Shareef
a soldier for
Allah

Patriarch, Activist & Humanitarian

Friends of the Pen

Now Available
www.innerchildpress.com/anthologies

Inner Child Press Anthologies

Now Available
www.innerchildpress.com

Inner Child Press Anthologies

I want my poetry to... volume 4

the conscious poets

inspired by ... Monte Smith

Now Available
www.innerchildpress.com/anthologies

Now Available
www.innerchildpress.com/anthologies

Inner Child Press Anthologies

Now Available
www.worldhealingworldpeacepoetry.com

Inner Child Press Anthologies

Now Available
www.innerchildpress.com/anthologies

Inner Child Press Anthologies

Now Available
www.worldhealingworldpeacepoetry.com

Inner Child Press Anthologies

Now Available
www.innerchildpress.com/anthologies

Inner Child Press Anthologies

Inner Child Press International
&
The Year of the Poet
present

Poetry
the best of 2020

Poets of the World

Now Available
www.innerchildpress.com/anthologies

Inner Child Press Anthologies

Now Available
www.innerchildpress.com/anthologies

Inner Child Press Anthologies

Now Available
www.innerchildpress.com/anthologies

Inner Child Press Anthologies

Now Available
www.innerchildpress.com/anthologies

Inner Child Press Anthologies

Now Available
www.innerchildpress.com/anthologies

Inner Child Press Anthologies

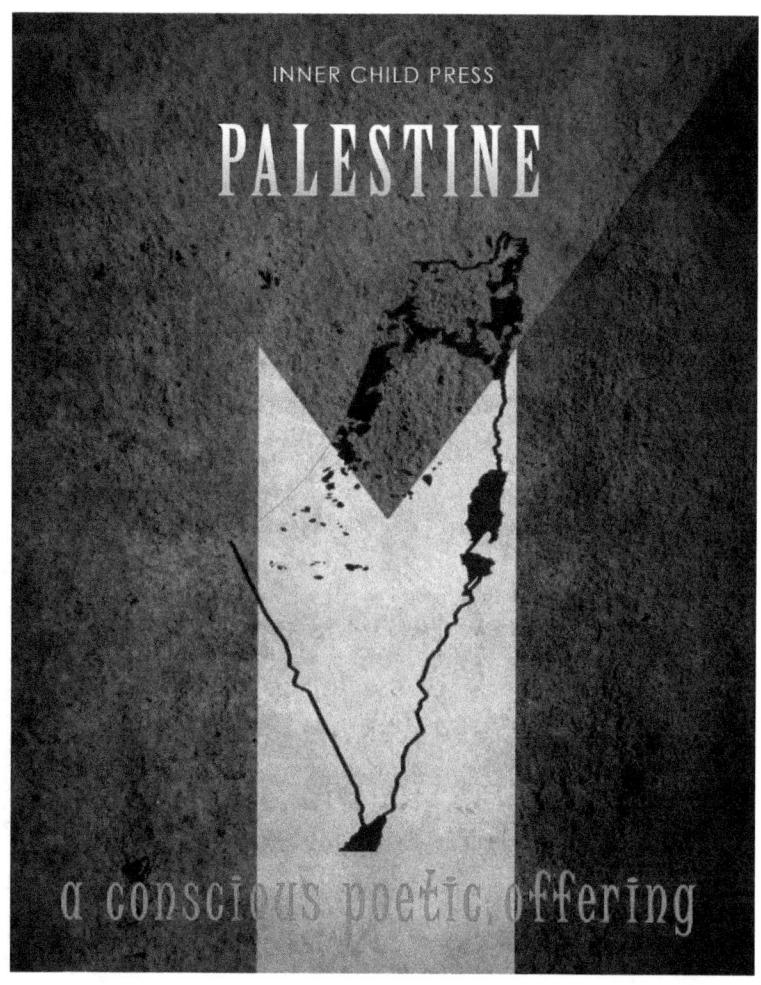

Now Available
www.innerchildpress.com/anthologies

Inner Child Press Anthologies

Now Available
www.innerchildpress.com/anthologies

Inner Child Press Anthologies

Now Available
www.innerchildpress.com/anthologies

Inner Child Press Anthologies

Now Available
www.worldhealingworldpeacepoetry.com

Inner Child Press Anthologies

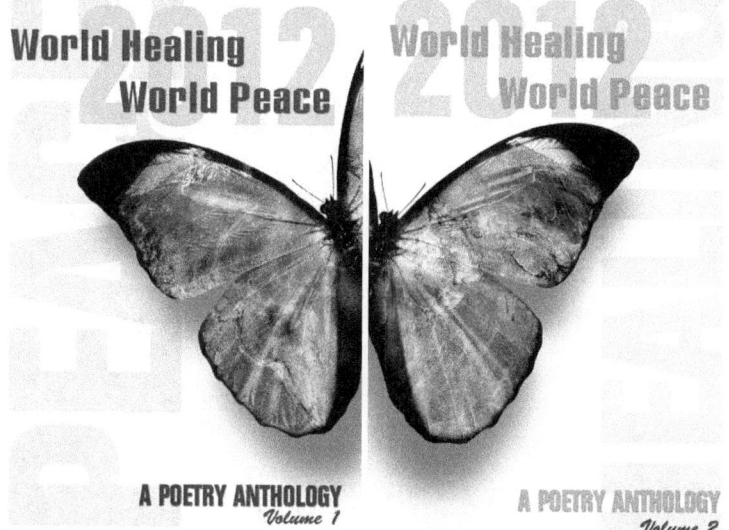

Now Available
www.worldhealingworldpeacepoetry.com

Inner Child Press Anthologies

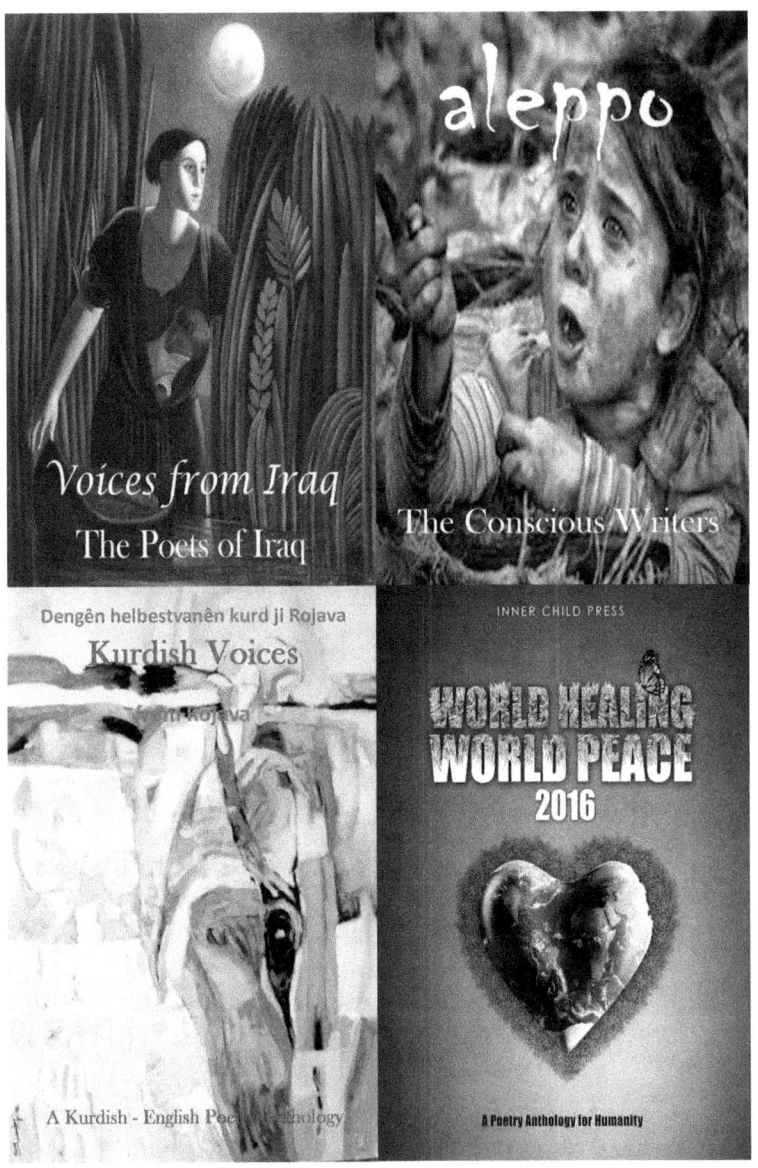

Now Available
www.innerchildpress.com/anthologies

Inner Child Press Anthologies

Now Available
www.innerchildpress.com/anthologies

Inner Child Press Anthologies

Now Available
www.innerchildpress.com/anthologies

Inner Child Press Anthologies

Now Available
www.innerchildpress.com/anthologies

Inner Child Press Anthologies

Now Available
www.innerchildpress.com/anthologies

Inner Child Press Anthologies

Now Available

www.innerchildpress.com/the-year-of-the-poet

Inner Child Press Anthologies

Now Available
www.innerchildpress.com/the-year-of-the-poet

Inner Child Press Anthologies

Now Available
www.innerchildpress.com/the-year-of-the-poet

Inner Child Press Anthologies

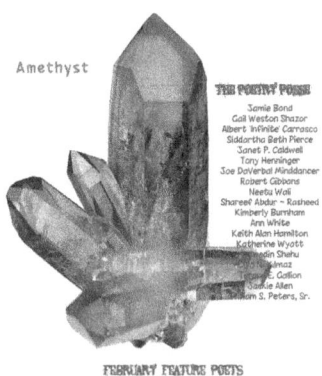

Now Available
www.innerchildpress.com/the-year-of-the-poet

Inner Child Press Anthologies

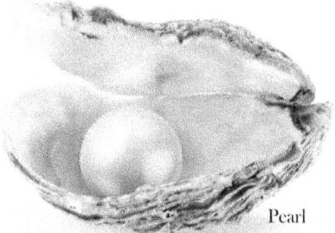

Now Available

www.innerchildpress.com/the-year-of-the-poet

Inner Child Press Anthologies

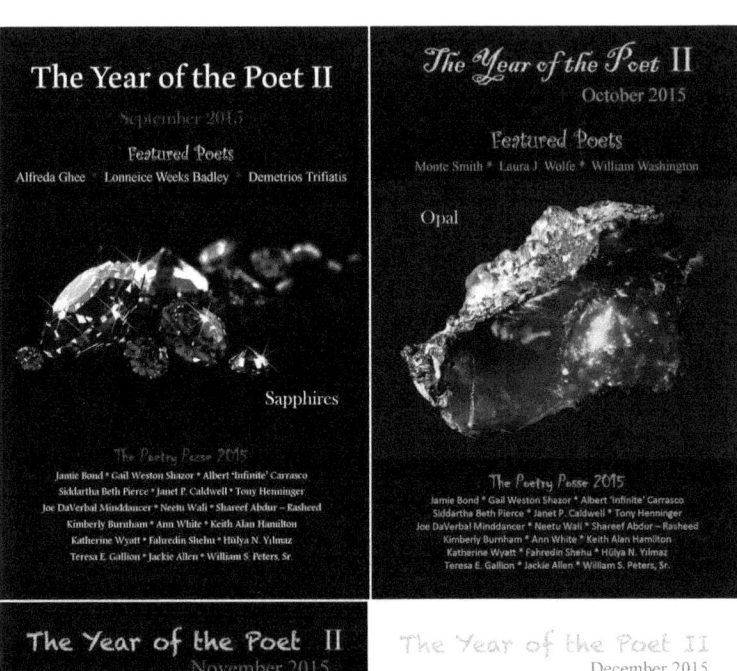

Now Available
www.innerchildpress.com/the-year-of-the-poet

Inner Child Press Anthologies

Now Available
www.innerchildpress.com/the-year-of-the-poet

Inner Child Press Anthologies

Now Available
www.innerchildpress.com/the-year-of-the-poet

Inner Child Press Anthologies

Now Available

www.innerchildpress.com/the-year-of-the-poet

Inner Child Press Anthologies

Now Available

www.innerchildpress.com/the-year-of-the-poet

Inner Child Press Anthologies

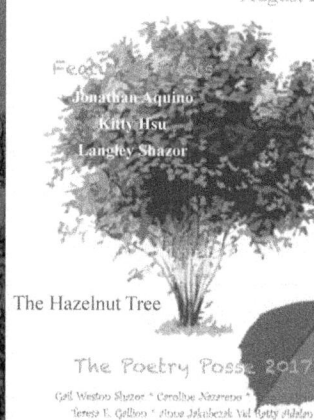

Now Available
www.innerchildpress.com/the-year-of-the-poet

Inner Child Press Anthologies

The Year of the Poet IV
September 2017

Featured Poets
Martina Reisz Newberry
Ameer Nassir
Christine Fulco Neal
Robert Neal

The Elm Tree

The Poetry Posse 2017

Gail Weston Shazor * Caroline Nazareno * Bismay Mohanty
Teresa E. Gallion * Anna Jakubczak Vel Ratty Adalan
Joe DaVerbal Minddancer * Shareef Abdur – Rasheed
Albert Carrasco * Kimberly Burnham * Elizabeth Castillo
Hülya N. Yılmaz * Faleeha Hassan * Jackie Davis Allen
Jen Walls * Nizar Sartawi * William S. Peters, Sr.

The Year of the Poet IV
October 2017

Featured Poets
Ahmed Abu Saleem
Nedal Al-Qaeim
Sadeddin Shahin

The Black Walnut Tree

The Poetry Posse 2017

Gail Weston Shazor * Caroline Nazareno * Bismay Mohanty
Teresa E. Gallion * Anna Jakubczak Vel Ratty Adalan
Joe DaVerbal Minddancer * Shareef Abdur – Rasheed
Albert Carrasco * Kimberly Burnham * Elizabeth Castillo
Hülya N. Yılmaz * Faleeha Hassan * Jackie Davis Allen
Jen Walls * Nizar Sartawi * * William S. Peters, Sr.

The Year of the Poet IV
November 2017

Featured Poets
Kay Peters
Alfreda D. Ghee
Gabriella Garofalo
Rosemary Cappello

The Tree of Life

The Poetry Posse 2017

Gail Weston Shazor * Caroline Nazareno * Bismay Mohanty
Teresa E. Gallion * Anna Jakubczak Vel Ratty Adalan
Joe DaVerbal Minddancer * Shareef Abdur – Rasheed
Albert Carrasco * Kimberly Burnham * Elizabeth Castillo
Hülya N. Yılmaz * Faleeha Hassan * Jackie Davis Allen
Jen Walls * Nizar Sartawi * William S. Peters, Sr.

The Year of the Poet IV
December 2017

Featured Poets
Justice Clarke
Mariel M. Pabroa
Kiley Brown

The Fig Tree

The Poetry Posse 2017

Gail Weston Shazor * Caroline Nazareno * Bismay Mohanty
Teresa E. Gallion * Anna Jakubczak Vel Ratty Adalan
Joe DaVerbal Minddancer * Shareef Abdur – Rasheed
Albert Carrasco * Kimberly Burnham * Elizabeth Castillo
Hülya N. Yılmaz * Faleeha Hassan * Jackie Davis Allen
Jen Walls * Nizar Sartawi * William S. Peters, Sr.

Now Available
www.innerchildpress.com/the-year-of-the-poet

Inner Child Press Anthologies

Now Available

www.innerchildpress.com/the-year-of-the-poet

Inner Child Press Anthologies

Now Available
www.innerchildpress.com/the-year-of-the-poet

Inner Child Press Anthologies

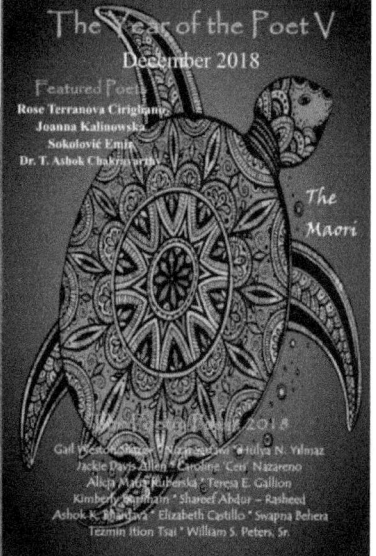

Now Available
www.innerchildpress.com/the-year-of-the-poet

Inner Child Press Anthologies

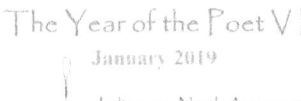

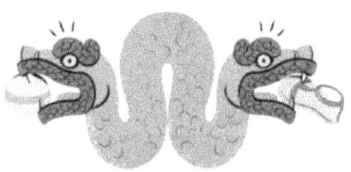
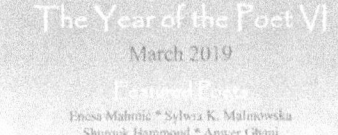

Now Available
www.innerchildpress.com/the-year-of-the-poet

Inner Child Press Anthologies

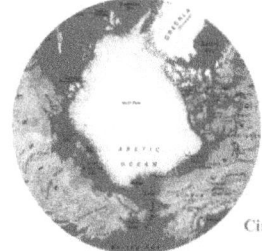

Now Available
www.innerchildpress.com/the-year-of-the-poet

Inner Child Press Anthologies

Now Available
www.innerchildpress.com/the-year-of-the-poet

Inner Child Press Anthologies

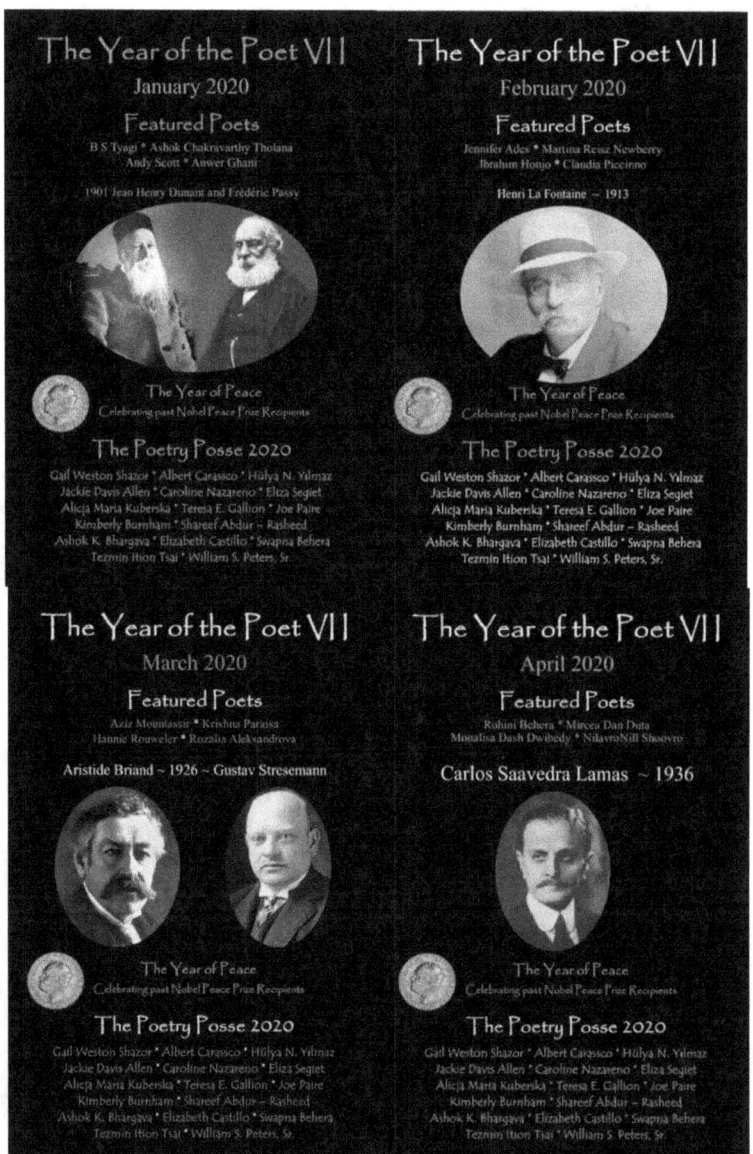

Now Available

www.innerchildpress.com/the-year-of-the-poet

Inner Child Press Anthologies

Now Available
www.innerchildpress.com/the-year-of-the-poet

Inner Child Press Anthologies

Now Available
www.innerchildpress.com/the-year-of-the-poet

Inner Child Press Anthologies

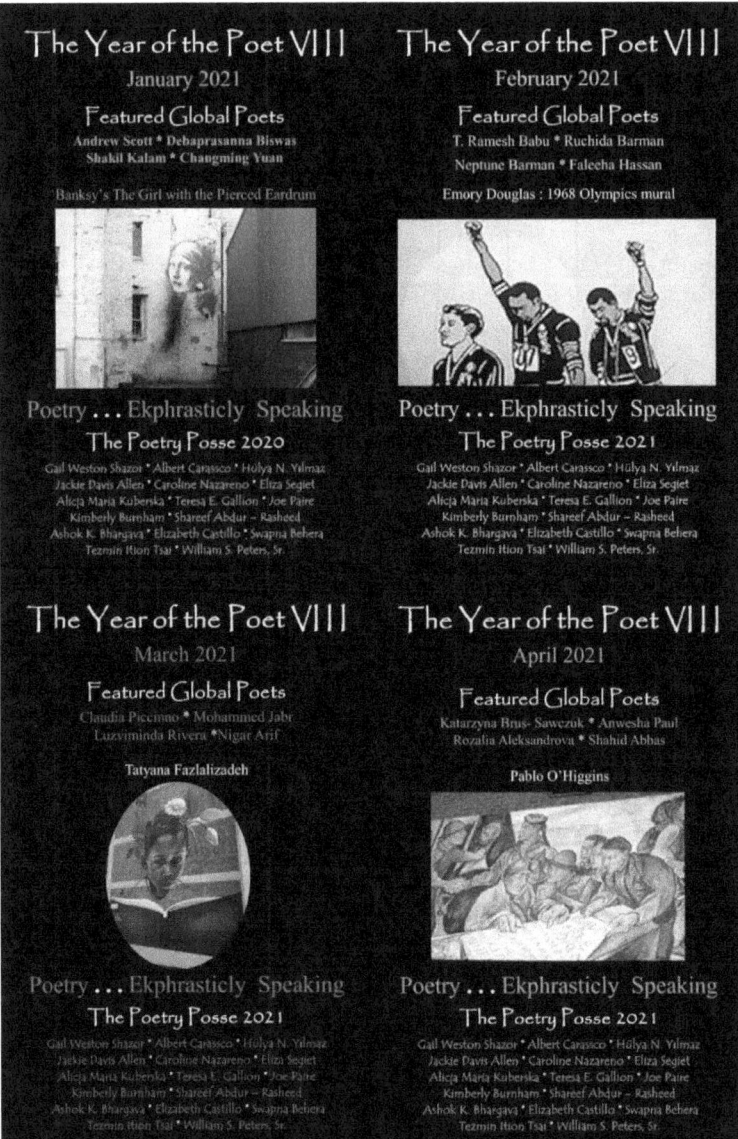

Now Available
www.innerchildpress.com/the-year-of-the-poet

Inner Child Press Anthologies

Now Available

www.innerchildpress.com/the-year-of-the-poet

Inner Child Press Anthologies

Now Available
www.innerchildpress.com/the-year-of-the-poet

Inner Child Press Anthologies

The Year of the Poet IX
January 2022

Featured Global Poets
**Ratan Ghosh * Christine Neil-Wright
Andrew Scott * Ashok Kumar**

Climate Change : The Ice Cap

Poetry . . . Ekphrasticly Speaking

The Poetry Posse 2021

Gail Weston Shazor * Albert Carasco * Hülya N. Yılmaz
Jackie Davis Allen * Caroline Nazareno * Eliza Segiet
Alicja Maria Kuberska * Teresa E. Gallion * Joe Paire
Kimberly Burnham * Shareef Abdur – Rasheed
Ashok K. Bhargava * Elizabeth Castillo * Swapna Behera
Tezmin Ition Tsai * William S. Peters, Sr.

The Year of the Poet IX
February 2022

Featured Global Poets
Roza Boyanova * Ramón de Jesús Núñez Duval
Mammad Ismayil * Tarana Turan Rahimli

Climate Change and Mountains

Poetry . . . Ekphrasticly Speaking

The Poetry Posse 2021

Gail Weston Shazor * Albert Carasco * Hülya N. Yılmaz
Jackie Davis Allen * Caroline Nazareno * Eliza Segiet
Alicja Maria Kuberska * Teresa E. Gallion * Joe Paire
Kimberly Burnham * Shareef Abdur – Rasheed
Ashok K. Bhargava * Elizabeth Castillo * Swapna Behera
Tezmin Ition Tsai * William S. Peters, Sr.

The Year of the Poet IX
March 2022

Featured Global Poets
Dimitris P. Kraniotis * Marlene Pasini
Kennedy Ochieng * Swayam Prashant

Climate Change and Space Debris

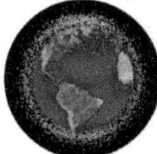

Poetry . . . Ekphrasticly Speaking

The Poetry Posse 2021

Gail Weston Shazor * Albert Carasco * Hülya N. Yılmaz
Jackie Davis Allen * Caroline Nazareno * Eliza Segiet
Alicja Maria Kuberska * Teresa E. Gallion * Joe Paire
Kimberly Burnham * Shareef Abdur – Rasheed
Ashok K. Bhargava * Elizabeth Castillo * Swapna Behera
Tezmin Ition Tsai * William S. Peters, Sr.

The Year of the Poet IX
April 2022

Featured Global Poets
**Alonzo Gross * Dr. Debaprasanna Biswas
Monsif Beroual * Carol Aronoff**

Climate Change and Oceans

*Celebrating our 100th Edition *

Poetry . . . Ekphrasticly Speaking

The Poetry Posse 2021

Gail Weston Shazor * Albert Carasco * Hülya N. Yılmaz
Jackie Davis Allen * Caroline Nazareno * Eliza Segiet
Alicja Maria Kuberska * Teresa E. Gallion * Joe Paire
Kimberly Burnham * Shareef Abdur – Rasheed
Ashok K. Bhargava * Elizabeth Castillo * Swapna Behera
Tezmin Ition Tsai * William S. Peters, Sr.

Now Available

www.innerchildpress.com/the-year-of-the-poet

Inner Child Press Anthologies

The Year of the Poet IX
May 2022

Featured Global Poets
Ndaba Sibanda * Smrutiranjan Mohanty
Ajanta Paul * Monalisa Dash Dwibedy

Climate Change and Birds

Poetry . . . Ekphrasticly Speaking

The Poetry Posse 2021

Gail Weston Shazor * Albert Carasco * Hülya N. Yılmaz
Jackie Davis Allen * Caroline Nazareno * Eliza Segiet
Alicja Maria Kuberska * Teresa E. Gallion * Joe Paire
Kimberly Burnham * Shareef Abdur – Rasheed
Ashok K. Bhargava * Elizabeth Castillo * Swapna Behera
Tezmin Ition Tsai * William S. Peters, Sr.

The Year of the Poet IX
June 2022

Featured Global Poets
Yuan Changming * Azeezat Okunlola
Tanja Ajtić * Philip Chijioke Abonyi

Climate Change and Trees

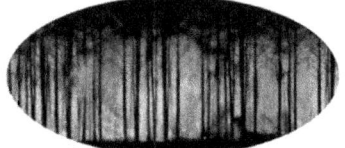

Poetry . . . Ekphrasticly Speaking

The Poetry Posse 2022

Gail Weston Shazor * Albert Carasco * Hülya N. Yılmaz
Jackie Davis Allen * Caroline Nazareno * Eliza Segiet
Alicja Maria Kuberska * Teresa E. Gallion * Joe Paire
Kimberly Burnham * Shareef Abdur – Rasheed
Ashok K. Bhargava * Elizabeth Castillo * Swapna Behera
Tezmin Ition Tsai * William S. Peters, Sr.

The Year of the Poet IX
July 2022

Featured Global Poets
Michelle Joan Barulich * Mili Das
Anna Ferriero * Ujjal Mandal

Climate Change and Animals

Poetry . . . Ekphrasticly Speaking

The Poetry Posse 2022

Gail Weston Shazor * Albert Carasco * Hülya N. Yılmaz
Jackie Davis Allen * Caroline Nazareno * Eliza Segiet
Alicja Maria Kuberska * Teresa E. Gallion * Joe Paire
Kimberly Burnham * Shareef Abdur – Rasheed
Ashok K. Bhargava * Elizabeth Castillo * Swapna Behera
Tezmin Ition Tsai * William S. Peters, Sr.

The Year of the Poet IX
August 2022

Featured Global Poets
Pankhuri Sinha * Abdulloh Abdumominov
Caroline Turunç * Tali Cohen Shabtai

Climate Change and Agriculture

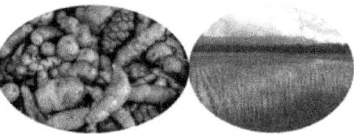

Poetry . . . Ekphrasticly Speaking

The Poetry Posse 2022

Gail Weston Shazor * Albert Carasco * Hülya N. Yılmaz
Jackie Davis Allen * Caroline Nazareno * Eliza Segiet
Alicja Maria Kuberska * Teresa E. Gallion * Joe Paire
Kimberly Burnham * Shareef Abdur – Rasheed
Ashok K. Bhargava * Elizabeth Castillo * Swapna Behera
Tezmin Ition Tsai * William S. Peters, Sr.

Now Available
www.innerchildpress.com/the-year-of-the-poet

Inner Child Press Anthologies

The Year of the Poet IX
September 2022

Featured Global Poets

Ngozi Olivia Osuoha * Biswajit Mishra
Sylwia K. Malinowska * Sajid Hussein

Climate Change and Wind and Weather Patterns

Poetry ... Ekphrasticly Speaking

The Poetry Posse 2022

Gail Weston Shazor * Albert Carasco * Hülya N. Yılmaz
Jackie Davis Allen * Caroline Nazareno * Eliza Segiet
Alicja Maria Kuberska * Teresa E. Gallion * Joe Paire
Kimberly Burnham * Shareef Abdur – Rasheed
Ashok K. Bhargava * Elizabeth Castillo * Swapna Behera
Tezmin Ition Tsai * William S. Peters, Sr.

The Year of the Poet IX
October 2022

Featured Global Poets

Andrew Kouroupos * Brenda Mohammed
Carthornia Kouroupos * Faleeha Hassan

Climate Change and Oil and Power

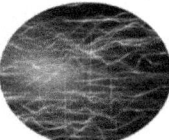 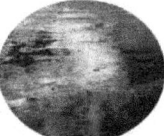

Poetry ... Ekphrasticly Speaking

The Poetry Posse 2022

Gail Weston Shazor * Albert Carasco * Hülya N. Yılmaz
Jackie Davis Allen * Caroline Nazareno * Eliza Segiet
Alicja Maria Kuberska * Teresa E. Gallion * Joe Paire
Kimberly Burnham * Shareef Abdur – Rasheed
Ashok K. Bhargava * Elizabeth Castillo * Swapna Behera
Tezmin Ition Tsai * William S. Peters, Sr.

The Year of the Poet IX
November 2022

Featured Global Poets

Henna Ravi * Shaffkat Aziz Hajam
Selma Kopic * Ibrahim Honjo

Climate Change : Time to Act

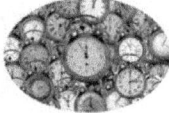 

Poetry ... Ekphrasticly Speaking

The Poetry Posse 2022

Gail Weston Shazor * Albert Carasco * Hülya N. Yılmaz
Jackie Davis Allen * Caroline Nazareno * Eliza Segiet
Alicja Maria Kuberska * Teresa E. Gallion * Joe Paire
Kimberly Burnham * Shareef Abdur – Rasheed
Ashok K. Bhargava * Elizabeth Castillo * Swapna Behera
Tezmin Ition Tsai * William S. Peters, Sr.

The Year of the Poet IX
December 2022

Featured Global Poets

Elarbi Abdelfattah * Lorraine Cragg
Neha Bhandarkar * Robert Gibbons

Climate Change Bees, Butterflies and Insect Life

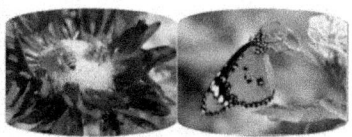

Poetry ... Ekphrasticly Speaking

The Poetry Posse 2022

Gail Weston Shazor * Albert Carasco * Hülya N. Yılmaz
Jackie Davis Allen * Caroline Nazareno * Eliza Segiet
Alicja Maria Kuberska * Teresa E. Gallion * Joe Paire
Kimberly Burnham * Shareef Abdur – Rasheed
Ashok K. Bhargava * Elizabeth Castillo * Swapna Behera
Tezmin Ition Tsai * William S. Peters, Sr.

Now Available

www.innerchildpress.com/the-year-of-the-poet

Now Available
www.innerchildpress.com/the-year-of-the-poet

Inner Child Press Anthologies

Now Available
www.innerchildpress.com/the-year-of-the-poet

Inner Child Press Anthologies

Now Available
www.innerchildpress.com/the-year-of-the-poet

Inner Child Press Anthologies

The Year of the Poet XI
January 2024

Featured Global Poets
Til Kumari Sharma * Shafkat Aziz Hajam
Daniela Marian * Eleni Vassiliou – Asteroskon

Renowned Poets

~ Phyllis Wheatley ~

The Poetry Posse 2024
Gail Weston Shazor * Albert Carasso * Hülya N. Yılmaz
Jackie Davis Allen * Caroline Nazareno * Mutawaf Shaheed
Alicja Maria Kuberska * Teresa E. Gallion * Noreen Snyder
Michelle Joan Barulich * Shareef Abdur – Rasheed
Ashok K. Bhargava * Elizabeth Castillo * Swapna Behera
Tezmin Ition Tsai * Eliza Segiet * William S. Peters, Sr.

The Year of the Poet XI
February 2024

Featured Global Poets
Caroline Laurent Turunç * Julio Pavanetti
Lidia Chiarelli * Lina Buividavičiūtė

Renowned Poets

~ Omar Khayyam ~

The Poetry Posse 2024
Gail Weston Shazor * Albert Carasso * Hülya N. Yılmaz
Jackie Davis Allen * Caroline Nazareno * Mutawaf Shaheed
Alicja Maria Kuberska * Teresa E. Gallion * Noreen Snyder
Michelle Joan Barulich * Shareef Abdur – Rasheed
Ashok K. Bhargava * Elizabeth Castillo * Swapna Behera
Tezmin Ition Tsai * Eliza Segiet * William S. Peters, Sr.

The Year of the Poet XI
March 2024

Featured Global Poets
Francesco Favetta * Jagjit Singh Zandu
Carmela Núñez Yukimura Peruana * Michael Lee Johnson

Renowned Poets

~ Nâzim Hikmet ~

The Poetry Posse 2024
Gail Weston Shazor * Albert Carasso * Hülya N. Yılmaz
Jackie Davis Allen * Caroline Nazareno * Mutawaf Shaheed
Alicja Maria Kuberska * Teresa E. Gallion * Noreen Snyder
Michelle Joan Barulich * Shareef Abdur – Rasheed
Ashok K. Bhargava * Elizabeth Castillo * Swapna Behera
Tezmin Ition Tsai * Eliza Segiet * William S. Peters, Sr.

The Year of the Poet XI
April 2024

Featured Global Poets
Hassanal Abdullah * Johny Takkedasila
Rajashree Mohapatra * Shirley Smothers

Renowned Poets

~ William Butler Yeats ~

The Poetry Posse 2024
Gail Weston Shazor * Albert Carasso * Hülya N. Yılmaz
Jackie Davis Allen * Caroline Nazareno * Mutawaf Shaheed
Alicja Maria Kuberska * Teresa E. Gallion * Noreen Snyder
Michelle Joan Barulich * Shareef Abdur – Rasheed
Ashok K. Bhargava * Elizabeth Castillo * Swapna Behera
Tezmin Ition Tsai * Eliza Segiet * William S. Peters, Sr.

Now Available

www.innerchildpress.com/the-year-of-the-poet

Inner Child Press Anthologies

The Year of the Poet XI
May 2024

Featured Global Poets
Binod Dawadi * Petros Kyriakou Veloudas
Rayees Ahmad Kumar * Solomon C Jatta

Renowned Poets

~ Makhanlal Chaturvedi ~

The Poetry Posse 2024

Gail Weston Shazor * Albert Carasco * Hülya N. Yılmaz
Jackie Davis Allen * Caroline Nazareno * Mutawaf Shaheed
Alicja Maria Kuberska * Teresa E. Gallion * Noreen Snyder
Michelle Joan Barulich * Shareef Abdur – Rasheed
Ashok K. Bhargava * Elizabeth Castillo * Swapna Behera
Tezmin Ition Tsai * Eliza Segiet * William S. Peters, Sr.

The Year of the Poet XI
June 2024

Featured Global Poets
C. S. P Shrivastava * Maria Evelyn Quilla Soleta
Moulay Cherif Chebihi Hassani * Swayam Prashant

Renowned Poets

~ Langston Hughs ~

The Poetry Posse 2024

Gail Weston Shazor * Albert Carasco * Hülya N. Yılmaz
Jackie Davis Allen * Caroline Nazareno * Mutawaf Shaheed
Alicja Maria Kuberska * Teresa E. Gallion * Noreen Snyder
Michelle Joan Barulich * Shareef Abdur – Rasheed
Ashok K. Bhargava * Elizabeth Castillo * Swapna Behera
Tezmin Ition Tsai * Eliza Segiet * William S. Peters, Sr.

The Year of the Poet XI
July 2024

Featured Global Poets
Barbara Gaiardoni * Bharati Nayak
Errol Bean * Michael Lee Johnson

Renowned Poets

~ Pablo Neruda ~

The Poetry Posse 2024

Gail Weston Shazor * Albert Carasco * Hülya N. Yılmaz
Jackie Davis Allen * Caroline Nazareno * Mutawaf Shaheed
Alicja Maria Kuberska * Teresa E. Gallion * Noreen Snyder
Michelle Joan Barulich * Shareef Abdur – Rasheed
Ashok K. Bhargava * Elizabeth Castillo * Swapna Behera
Tezmin Ition Tsai * Eliza Segiet * William S. Peters, Sr.

The Year of the Poet XI
August 2024

Featured Global Poets
Ibrahim Honjo * Khalice Jade
Irma Kurti * Mennadi Farah

Renowned Poets

~ Li Bai ~

The Poetry Posse 2024

Gail Weston Shazor * Albert Carasco * Hülya N. Yılmaz
Jackie Davis Allen * Caroline Nazareno * Mutawaf Shaheed
Alicja Maria Kuberska * Teresa E. Gallion * Noreen Snyder
Michelle Joan Barulich * Shareef Abdur – Rasheed
Ashok K. Bhargava * Elizabeth Castillo * Swapna Behera
Tezmin Ition Tsai * Eliza Segiet * William S. Peters, Sr.

Now Available

www.innerchildpress.com/the-year-of-the-poet

Inner Child Press Anthologies

The Year of the Poet XI
September 2024

Featured Global Poets

Ngozi Olivia Osuoha * Teodozja Świderska
Chinh Nguyen * Awatef El Idrissi Boukhris

Renowned Poets

~ William Ernest Henley ~

The Poetry Posse 2024

Gail Weston Shazor * Albert Carasco * Hülya N. Yılmaz
Jackie Davis Allen * Caroline Nazareno * Mutawaf Shaheed
Alicja Maria Kuberska * Teresa E. Gallion * Noreen Snyder
Michelle Joan Barulich * Shareef Abdur – Rasheed
Ashok K. Bhargava * Elizabeth Castillo * Swapna Behera
Tezmin Ition Tsai * Eliza Segiet * William S. Peters, Sr.

The Year of the Poet XI
October 2024

Featured Global Poets

Deepak Kumar Dey * Shallal 'Anouz
Adnan Al-Sayegh * Taghrid Bou Merhi

Renowned Poets

~ Adam Mickiewicz ~

The Poetry Posse 2024

Gail Weston Shazor * Albert Carasco * Hülya N. Yılmaz
Jackie Davis Allen * Caroline Nazareno * Mutawaf Shaheed
Alicja Maria Kuberska * Teresa E. Gallion * Noreen Snyder
Michelle Joan Barulich * Shareef Abdur – Rasheed
Ashok K. Bhargava * Elizabeth Castillo * Swapna Behera
Tzemin Ition Tsai * Eliza Segiet * William S. Peters, Sr.

The Year of the Poet XI
November 2024

Featured Global Poets

Abraham Tawiah Tei * Neha Bhandarkar
Zaneta Varnado Johns * Haseena Bnaiyan

Renowned Poets

~ Wole Soyinka ~

The Poetry Posse 2024

Gail Weston Shazor * Albert Carasco * Hülya N. Yılmaz
Jackie Davis Allen * Caroline Nazareno * Mutawaf Shaheed
Alicja Maria Kuberska * Teresa E. Gallion * Noreen Snyder
Michelle Joan Barulich * Shareef Abdur – Rasheed
Ashok K. Bhargava * Elizabeth Castillo * Swapna Behera
Tezmin Ition Tsai * Eliza Segiet * William S. Peters, Sr.

The Year of the Poet XI
December 2024

Featured Global Poets

Kapardeli Eftichia * Irena Jovanović
Sudipta Mishra * Til Kumari Sharma

Renowned Poets

~ Imru' al-Qais ~

The Poetry Posse 2024

Gail Weston Shazor * Albert Carasco * Hülya N. Yılmaz
Jackie Davis Allen * Caroline Nazareno * Mutawaf Shaheed
Alicja Maria Kuberska * Teresa E. Gallion * Noreen Snyder
Michelle Joan Barulich * Shareef Abdur – Rasheed * Swapna Behera
Ashok K. Bhargava * Elizabeth Castillo * Kimberly Burnham
Tzemin Ition Tsai * Eliza Segiet * William S. Peters, Sr.

Now Available

www.innerchildpress.com/the-year-of-the-poet

Inner Child Press Anthologies

Now Available
www.innerchildpress.com/the-year-of-the-poet

Inner Child Press Anthologies

The Year of the Poet XII
May 2025

Featured Global Poets

Swayam Prashant * Ngozi Olivia Osuoha
Kazimierz Burnat * Deepak Kumar Dey

Bittersweetness	Empathy	Sadness
Bittersweetness	Lillies	Sunflowers

The Poetry Posse 2025

Gail Weston Shazor * Albert Carasso * Hülya N. Yılmaz
Jackie Davis Allen * Caroline Nazareno * Mutawaf Shaheed
Alicja Maria Kuberska * Teresa E. Gallion * Noreen Snyder
Shareef Abdur – Rasheed * Swapna Behera * Eliza Segiet
Ashok K. Bhargava * Elizabeth Castillo * Kimberly Burnham
Tzemin Ition Tsai * William S. Peters, Sr.

The Year of the Poet XII
June 2025

Featured Global Poets

Ayham Mahmoud Al-Abbad * Til Kumari Sharma
Michael Lee Johnson * Sylwia K. Malinowska

Love	Gratitude	Contentment
Red Roses	Blue Hydrangea	Azure Bluets

The Poetry Posse 2025

Gail Weston Shazor * Albert Carasso * Hülya N. Yılmaz
Jackie Davis Allen * Caroline Nazareno * Mutawaf Shaheed
Alicja Maria Kuberska * Teresa E. Gallion * Noreen Snyder
Shareef Abdur – Rasheed * Swapna Behera * Eliza Segiet
Ashok K. Bhargava * Elizabeth Castillo * Kimberly Burnham
Tzemin Ition Tsai * William S. Peters, Sr.

The Year of the Poet XII
July 2025

Featured Global Poets

Mennadi Farah * Aklima Ankhi
Niloy Rafiq * Petros Kyriakou Veloudas

Nostalgia	Wisdom	Fearlessness
Lillacs	Purple Iris	Gladiolas

The Poetry Posse 2025

Gail Weston Shazor * Albert Carasso * Hülya N. Yılmaz
Jackie Davis Allen * Caroline Nazareno * Mutawaf Shaheed
Alicja Maria Kuberska * Teresa E. Gallion * Noreen Snyder
Shareef Abdur – Rasheed * Swapna Behera * Eliza Segiet
Ashok K. Bhargava * Elizabeth Castillo * Kimberly Burnham
Tzemin Ition Tsai * William S. Peters, Sr.

The Year of the Poet XII
August 2025

Featured Global Poets

Ivan Pozzoni * Ram Krishna Singh
Ibrahim Honjo * Kazimierz Burnat

Connection	Fulfillment	Hope
Sunflower	Lotus	Daffodils

The Poetry Posse 2025

Gail Weston Shazor * Albert Carasso * Hülya N. Yılmaz
Jackie Davis Allen * Caroline Nazareno * Mutawaf Shaheed
Alicja Maria Kuberska * Teresa E. Gallion * Noreen Snyder
Shareef Abdur – Rasheed * Swapna Behera * Eliza Segiet
Ashok K. Bhargava * Elizabeth Castillo * Kimberly Burnham
Tzemin Ition Tsai * William S. Peters, Sr.

Now Available

www.innerchildpress.com/the-year-of-the-poet

and there is much, much more !

visit . . .

www.innerchildpress.com/anthologies-sales-special.php

Also check out our Authors and all the wonderful Books Available at :

www.innerchildpress.com/authors-pages

Inner Child Press Anthologies

Now Available

www.worldhealingworldpeacepoetry.com

Inner Child Press Anthologies

Now Available

www.worldhealingworldpeacepoetry.com

Inner Child Press Anthologies

Now Available

www.worldhealingworldpeacepoetry.com

Inner Child Press Anthologies

Now Available

www.worldhealingworldpeacepoetry.com

World Healing World Peace

2012, 2014, 2016, 2018, 2020, 2022, 2024

Now Available

www.worldhealingworldpeacepoetry.com

Inner Child Press International

'building bridges of cultural understanding'

Meet the Board of Directors

William S. Peters, Sr.
Chair Person
Founder
Inner Child Enterprises
Inner Child Press

Hülya N Yılmaz
Director
Editing Services
Co-Chair Person

Fahredin B. Shehu
Director
Cultural Affairs

Elizabeth E. Castillo
Director
Recording Secretary

De'Andre Hawthorne
Director
Performance Poetry

Gail Weston Shazor
Director
Anthologies

Kimberly Burnham
Director
Cultural Ambassador
Pacific Northwest
USA

Ashok K. Bhargava
Director
WIN Awards

Deborah Smart
Director
Publicity
Marketing

Khalice Jade
Director
Translation
Services

www.innerchildpress.com

This Anthological Publication
is underwritten solely by

Inner Child Press International

Inner Child Press is a Publishing Company Founded and Operated by Writers. Our personal publishing experiences provides us an intimate understanding of the sometimes daunting challenges Writers, New and Seasoned may face in the Business of Publishing and Marketing their Creative "Written Work".

For more Information

Inner Child Press International

www.innerchildpress.com

'building bridges of cultural understanding'
202 Wiltree Court, State College, Pennsylvania 16801
www.innerchildpress.com

This is our world...

~ fini ~

www.ingramcontent.com/pod-product-compliance
Lightning Source LLC
LaVergne TN
LVHW051041080426
835508LV00019B/1644